The Doll Collection

The Doll Collection

Poems

Edited by Diane Lockward

Terrapin Books

© 2016 by Diane Lockward

Printed in the United States of America.
All rights reserved.

No part of this book may be reproduced in any manner, except for brief quotations embodied in critical articles or reviews.

Terrapin Books
4 Midvale Avenue
West Caldwell, New Jersey 07006

ISBN: 978-0-9969871-0-3
LCCN: 2015918324

First Edition

www.terrapinbooks.com

Cover Photograph by Emanuele Mazzoni
From the Antique Toy and Doll Museum in Provence, France, L'Isle sur la Sorgue

www.emanuelemazzoni.com

For All the Doll Lovers

Contents

Introduction / *Nicole Cooley*	1
Losses / *Dori Appel*	7
Dream Doll in the Making / *Jeanne Marie Beaumont*	8
The Family / *Chana Bloch*	9
Creosote / *Meg Hurtado Bloom*	10
Paper Dolls / *Paula Bohince*	11
Guardian / *Karina Borowicz*	12
Chewed-On Barbie / *Kim Bridgford*	13
The Doll Maker's Wife / *Jason Lee Brown*	14
In the Chair Museum / *Leah Browning*	15
The Model of Perfection / *Lauren Camp*	17
The Afterlife / *Neil Carpathios*	19
Marriage Doll / *Luanne Castle*	20
Puppet World / *Robin Chapman*	21
On the Work Ethic / *Kelly Cherry*	23
The Secret Lives of Little Girls / *Christopher Citro*	24
Doll Suitcase / *Geraldine Connolly*	25
The Pregnant Doll / *Nicole Cooley*	27
Because a Matryoshka Doll Is a Nest Made of Eggs / *Gillian Cummings*	28
The Doll Maker / *Laura E. Davis*	29
Frozen Charlotte / *Susan de Sola*	30
The Golem / *Jessica de Koninck*	31

The Room at the House in Croton / *Lori Desrosiers*	32
The Doll Museum / *Caitlyn Doyle*	34
Florida Doll Sonnet / *Denise Duhamel* and *Maureen Seaton*	35
In the Milk House / *Jane Ebihara*	36
Colleen Moore's Doll House / *Susan Elbe*	38
How to Hold on to the Magic of Fathers / *Patricia Fargnoli*	41
Metal Doll / *Roberta Feins*	42
The Rat Doll / *Ann Fisher-Wirth*	44
Snake Ladies / *Ann Fisher-Wirth*	45
Dolls for Sale / *Kelly Fordon*	46
I Go Back to the Doll Hospital / *Kerri French*	47
The Doll / *Alice Friman*	48
Doll Heads / *Richard Garcia*	51
What the Children Know / *Christine Gelineau*	53
Pretty Baby / *Gail Fishman Gerwin*	55
My Mother's Doll / *Meredith Davies Hadaway*	56
Unfound Love Note / *Marj Hahne*	57
Operation Teddy Bear / *Jeffrey Harrison*	58
Bad Times Barbie / *Donna Hilbert*	60
Carriage / *Akua Lezli Hope*	61
Plié / *Karla Huston*	62
Alan Doll Rap / *Julie Kane*	63
Cloth Doll with Found Feathers / *Susan Kelly-DeWitt*	65
Ginny / *Adele Kenny*	67
The Way It Broke / *Laurie Kolp*	68
Scary Movie / *Lori Lamothe*	69

Behind the Glass / *Jessica Wiseman Lawrence*	70
Paper Doll Ghazal / *Christina Lovin*	71
Delaware Guardian Doll / *Denise Low*	72
Bambi / *Mary Makofske*	73
After Torrential Rain / *Charlotte Mandel*	74
Still Lovers / *Jennifer Matteson*	76
Little Doll / *Joan Mazza*	78
Paper Doll / *Susan Laughter Meyers*	79
The Doll Handler Tells the Truth about Them / *Kristine Ong Muslim*	80
Dollhouse / *Gail Newman*	81
The Only House in the Neighborhood / *Sarah Rose Nordgren*	82
When You Ask Whether I Ever Played with Dolls / *Jennifer Perrine*	83
Pediophilia / *Jessica Piazza*	85
Every Body She Carries / *Andrea Potos*	86
Playing Drunks at Age 7 / *Kyle Potvin*	87
The Fear of Puppets and the Fear of Beautiful Women / *Jendi Reiter*	88
Potato Head / *Susan Rich*	90
This Child Left / *Susanna Rich*	92
The Apothecary Doll / *Kim Roberts*	93
Sonnenizio on a Line from Ciardi / *Marybeth Rua-Larsen*	95
Flip Doll: Red Riding Hood / *Hayden Saunier*	96
The Promise / *Enid Shomer*	97
I Hit My Sister Across the Back with the Speak-n-Spell / *Lauren Goodwin Slaughter*	99

17th Century Ivory Anatomical Model / *Emma Sovich*	101
When Catholics Believed in Limbo / *Mary Ellen Talley*	102
Secrets / *Elaine Terranova*	103
Broken Doll / *Susan Terris*	104
How Dolls Are Made / *Maria Terrone*	105
American Girl / *Marjorie Tesser*	106
Her Garden / *J. C. Todd*	107
Dresden China Boy / *Carine Topal*	109
Madame Alexander's Amy / *Alison Townsend*	110
Playing with Dolls / *David Trinidad*	112
To Be Blameless Is to Be Miniature / *Lee Upton*	114
Burning the Dolls / *Michael Waters*	115
A Shelter of Dolls / *Ingrid Wendt*	117
Playing GI Joes / *Scott Wiggerman*	118
The Stolen Girl / *George Witte*	119
Burning the Doll / *Cecilia Woloch*	120
The Doll Mother / *Kristin Camitta Zimet*	122
Foresight / *Theodora Ziolkowski*	123
Contributors	125
Credits	137
About the Editor	143

*Nothing that grieves us can be called little:
by the eternal laws of proportion a child's loss
of a doll and a king's loss of a crown are events
of the same size.*
—Mark Twain

*There's nobody else that can double me—
except for a doll.*
—Verne Troyer

Introduction

For hours, I studied all the dolls on display. I had wandered into the Victoria and Albert Museum of Childhood, in Bethanel Green, London, and I could not believe how many dolls were collected there. Case after case. A Mutton Bone Doll. A Paddle Doll Made in Egypt. A Two-faced Doll with a crying mechanism lodged deep in her body. One of the very first Barbies from 1959. A Flirting Eyed Doll that blew fake kisses. A row of tiny Frozen Charlottes, hands touching. I was transfixed. I found myself writing down the dolls' names and dates and descriptions in my notebook, taking photographs, wanting to preserve their images, wanting to keep them with me. I was enthralled.

Seeing all the dolls at once, together in this museum, all the dolls from different places and eras, all the dolls with different histories and stories made me ask: Why do dolls compel us so much? What are their meanings? What lessons do they have to teach us?

The Doll Collection explores these questions. This wonderful anthology of poems Diane Lockward has edited asks us to rethink dolls. Not just toys, dolls signify much more than childhood. Dolls shape our thinking about the female body, about race and class. Dolls influence our understanding of childhood. Symbols of perfection, they both comfort and terrify. Dolls represent as Freud would say—through E.T.A. Hoffman—the "uncanny." They are replicas, simulacra, souvenirs and secrets. They are objects we recall with intense nostalgia but also bodies we dismember and destroy. They might be made of cornhusks, clay, rags, paper, cloth, wood, porcelain, celluloid, bisque, plastic, or metal.

The genealogies and histories of dolls are endlessly fascinating. While some say "Doll" originates from the nickname for "Dorothy," others trace its origin back to the Greek word *edilon,* meaning "idol." In his book *The Art of Small Things* (Harvard University Press, 2007), art historian John Mack notes that the connection between "idol" and "doll" is important if not etymologically direct. He explains that "the word *doll* is a relatively recent invention" and observes that only at the beginning of the eighteenth century did the word come to acquire its current meaning. But Mack notes, "The original overlap of meaning between something played with innocently and something manipulated with intent remains a part of its total context." That paradoxical set of meanings is key to our understanding of dolls.

In "Playing with Dolls Isn't Just Fun and Games," a 2015 essay in the online magazine *Racked,* Hayley Krischer argues that dolls have always had an important pedagogical purpose which even expands beyond teaching caretaking: "In the 1700s and 1800s, for instance, rag dolls were used to teach sewing skills. Funeral dolls or Victorian mourning dolls helped children deal with high infant mortality rates, or served as an after-life keepsake with which a family could bury their child. It was only since the early 1900s that wax-head baby dolls, imported from England, were made to resemble babies as opposed to adults." For centuries, dolls have taught us how to understand our world.

Dolls are innocent. Dolls are tools of manipulation. Dolls are teaching tools. Yet dolls are all of this and at the same time none. The poems in *The Doll Collection,* the first anthology of poems to focus on dolls, investigate all of these meanings and more. The poems in this book take place in the spaces where dolls exist: homes, doll hospitals, toy stores, playrooms, workrooms. Poems are told from the point of view of dolls, doll owners, parents, children, doll makers, speakers who wish they were dolls. Many of the poems are about family—not only mothers and grandmothers and sisters, but also brothers, fathers, and grandfathers.

A Speak-n-Spell doll. Raggedy Ann. Matryoshka dolls that open to hold others. A rat doll. GI Joe. A red riding hood flip doll that is both girl and her grandma. Throughout the book, poems look at all these dolls from many different perspectives and tell many different stories. A new baby daughter is treated like a doll after a mother's stillbirth. A Ginny doll and her handmade furniture stay safe behind glass years after a father's death. When no one in the house is awake, a boy sneaks downstairs to play with his sister's Barbies. A doll maker builds a fifteen-inch doll to replace his wife. Frozen Charlotte dies of cold, then floats in a child's bath.

Dolls are smashed and broken. Dolls are set on fire. Dolls are repaired. Dolls are lost and then recovered. Dolls often appear in dreams. Representing dolls through many forms, the anthology includes prose poems, a ghazal, a rap, a number of sonnets—and a sonnenizio!—a sestina, and even a collaborative poem.

I have always thought that dolls and poems are a natural combination. Ever since I was a child, my dolls were part of my writing, as I arranged them into orphanages with my sister and wrote my own stories and poems about them. Now, I love to bring images of dolls to my poetry workshops for writing exercises. I bring my many books on dolls and doll collecting and my postcards from doll museums I've visited.

At first, my students are dubious, reluctant, and even uncomfortable, disbelieving that dolls will offer them anything new to work through in their writing. Dolls are childish things they believe they've put away. Then I pass out my images and we begin writing, describing the doll, writing from its point of view, writing from the point of view of someone who made the doll, someone who destroyed it. And the poems my students write always amaze all of us with their uncanny, strange, frightening, and beautiful images. Dolls take us to new unexpected places.

The Doll Collection shows us that dolls are windows to other worlds.

Dolls are portals to our pasts and to ourselves.

Dolls open the doors to our imagination.

Nicole Cooley

Losses

This dream was of our Raggedy Anns,
comparing scars and losses. Yours
showed her face grotesquely smooth
all down the left-hand side, where
wild Kim bit off one shoe-button eye
the year we lived on Barbados. Mine
cringed beneath her strange disguise,
the wig of honey-colored sausage curls
that Grandma bought at Woolworth's
to hide the scraps of ragged yarn
after I cut off the rest.

In my dream I was searching for
the missing yarn and button
when Kim came scampering in,
her thin legs spotted with gentian violet,
her fist closed tight. Then Walt,
the building's janitor when I was eight,
appeared from somewhere, his hands
grimy with basement coal dust,
coal dust on his overalls and cap.

As he grabbed my doll, I woke
with my heart pounding and
crossed the hall to your room,
tripping in the dark over your
clothes and books. For a long time
I sat in the rocker near your bed,
while I thought about our
Raggedy Anns and their bad luck,
my breathing slowing down
to match your sleeping breath.

—Dori Appel

Dream Doll in the Making

The burden summoned from the drawer.
She found the doll there, and
discarded the legs.
She gathered tools: wire cutters, soldering iron, awl.
Also, sponge moss, polymer clay, rusty pins, fiberfill.
She put a bird in her hand.
She used her favorite glue.
She reattached her hair and added millinery flowers.
A bit of traction to improve the neck.
She placed her on a silver platter.
Something waited for her beneath the surface.
She slept with the rumors, with the numinous.
She embraced her refusal to fail.
She found some free lace, that had survived
a fire, untouched by smoke.
She learned one joke: Why did Dracula visit the dress shop?
There were minor final embellishments:
    such as the weaving of danger,
    the stamping of words
    the construction of character X 7.
She named her Serendipity-do.
She became a *continuously floating thing*.
A fishbowl notoriety followed her everywhere.
Against the elements, she fared well.
Her husband came in handy and
just in time
to revamp her wardrobe.

                              —*Jeanne Marie Beaumont*

The Family

Inside the Russian woman there's
a carved doll,
red and yellow to match her,
with its own child inside.
The smallest, light as a saltshaker,
holds nothing
but a finger's breadth of emptiness.

Every morning we are lifted
out of each other,
arms stiff at our sides.
In the shock of daylight
we see our own
varnished faces everywhere.

At night we drop back
into each other's darkness.
A tight round sky
closes over us
like a candle snuffer.

We sleep
staring at the inside.

—*Chana Bloch*

Creosote

for my sister

We breezed in tiny nighties through larders and parks
and knee-high fields dotted only by the Indian dead.

We dismissed all our punishments,
planned the plastic futures of hundreds of dolls,

each flaking veil of paint steadily revealing
what it means to be a woman.

We sentenced them to barren frontiers, compulsive affairs
that arose and were cut down like zombies in their prime.

Some nights the desert blazed pink as our Barbie jeep
and then went out like an unbeloved nightlight.

Our mother hollered but we kept very quiet, let the sand
imprint deep into our knees, get dark, and seep dew.

Had we grown up amid fireflies, the promise of snow,
we might not have learned that staying away

is always the answer. Even so, yours is the love
that taught me to speak, that follows me home.

—Meg Hurtado Bloom

Paper Dolls

> *The Dionne quintuplets and their government-run nursery, "Quintland," became a major tourist attraction in Canada in the 1930s. The sisters' likenesses adorned paper dolls and other souvenirs.*

Little notes harmonizing
in a hope chest, in a shoebox willed
by the auntie who took in
laundry, never marrying, staying chaste
and bleached and burning.

These girls flirt easily (cheeky
dumplings), brunette curls of each
Dionne drawn differently, distinguishing
Annette from Emilie, Yvonne
from Cécile and Marie.

Touching, the doilies
Anna cut long as christening dresses,
pasting lace over nude
and dimpled limbs, the pastel
layettes they were born in.

Each quint given a life, made
bride, clasped in cardboard and cedar,
good and attentive as their true
counterparts were, amusing millions
through gauze and wire.

—Paula Bohince

Guardian

A tiny animal kept close to me on a string.
Warm and precious wool, a little black lamb whose face
is a miniature universe. Then the dream
shifts, I'm walking along my childhood beach
and there's a doll's arm in a nest of seaweed,
a leg pokes from the parted mouth of a blue
quahog shell. Keep walking. A doll's red-cheeked
face, golden curls tumbling in the foam
that pumps in and out at the shore like the edge
of a huge heart. But it's not up to me to put
the doll together. It's understood: I'm here to guard
separation, preside over the widening drift.

—*Karina Borowicz*

Chewed-On Barbie

There's something in perfection that calls out
To be destroyed. Rome, youth, fame, innocence:
There's all the plastic paradise of surface,
All the ways that, once you're chewed, you're not

The person you once were. You have more friends
Now that you're more like them, look off in space,
Warn them, again, of terror, offer mace.
They like that you're brought low, the loosened strands
From the ponytail that whipped its sculpted end.

But what was not predicted: some men's marrow
Thrills at what's been chewed-on, and that sorrow.
A woman who loves Cabernet, you lend
The vulnerability of brokenness.
They recognize it as their home address.

—Kim Bridgford

The Doll Maker's Wife

When my wife tried to leave, she said,
"This time it's final." I was at my workbench,
about to drill a fifteen-inch woman
in a vice, unmindful to all but doll making.
With the neck clamped tight, I bored into her
hipbone and sawed below the wooden breast,
grabbed a partial torso from the drawer,
then dumped a bucket of arms and legs
across the scarred workbench. I loved
rummaging through the tiny hands and feet,
hundreds in several shapes and sizes,
separated in cardboard boxes, searching
for the perfect set to replace my wife.

—Jason Lee Brown

In the Chair Museum

On Christmas Day, we drove north
to spend the afternoon with friends.

I was homesick for New Mexico
and brought biscochitos in the shape of stars.

We all walked to Montara State Beach
where it was cold and windy and beautiful

and watched the sun set like a piece of golden glass
over the ocean. I couldn't believe it was truly

December. On the way back to the house,
I held his little mitten in my gloved hand.

He was getting older and it felt like the last time
this might happen, like I needed to remember it.

We took the longest route and stopped to look
at strings of Christmas lights in the front yards.

By the time we returned, the men had built
a fire in a metal bowl on the back porch.

Later, after dinner, I looked through a book
with one of the boys, a very thick book about chairs.

He sat close to me on the couch and I wanted time
to stop for a moment so we could go on forever

turning page after page of glossy color photographs
of all the different colors and types of chairs.

Christmas ended, and New Year's. The book dissolved,
all of it did, as though it had never happened.

A few months later, I dreamed that I was a doll,
walking on my little legs through the chair museum.

Next door was the table museum, and on the other side
of it was the spoon museum, and so on. You get the idea.

The chairs in my museum were very large,
and I felt so small as I walked between them.

I wasn't sure why I was there, or what I was supposed to be
learning, but I knew that I had to be there for a reason.

So all night, I walked around in my little stockings and
my little black felt slippers with the straps across the tops.

All night, I walked around and around the museum,
peeking up at chairs through my little glass eyes,

certain that all of the answers were right there in front of me
if only I knew where to look.

—Leah Browning

The Model of Perfection

My sister poured over into sleep
each night, her family of dolls lined up

around her in the red room,
and when they pushed into channels

of the twin bed
with their ecstatic colors, she responded

with patience for her dolls,
never worried

about the stuffed heads
and how their brains seemed to slip out

in threads and jumbled cloth,
or about the hairline cracks in the ceramic faces

or the way limbs jointed in all directions,
twisted

and dangling. She endured
the dead-white skin

and listened as their carved, painted mouths
clamped down on their stories.

She preferred silence,
my sister. For her, it was enough

that their big heads towered over flimsy bodies.
She squeezed

her dolls into corners,
and each night as the air unzipped

with its tarnished breath in the eyeful dark,
her brown eyes looked into

glass eyes and whispered *good night*
to dozens of pursed lips.

—Lauren Camp

The Afterlife

Two boys found her on the beach
and started performing surgery,
popping out glassy eyes,
unscrewing the head.
Others noticed and huddled close
to watch. The boys let a little girl
with a striking resemblance
take the head and she sat
under an umbrella pulling a comb
through long blond hair.
A seagull swooped, plucked
an eyeball that rolled away.
The arms came off.
The boys stuck them in sand
so it looked as if
a buried person were clawing
her way up from deep
in the earth.
They threw legs back
and someone's dog dived into surf
fetching one, which made
everyone laugh.
Then the sun sank.
Nobody stayed.
Waves kept rolling.
All that remained was the torso
like a space craft or an ark,
which nobody wanted,
but soon small creatures
arrived, arm and leg sockets
round doors
for easy access and escape.

—*Neil Carpathios*

Marriage Doll

I spotted it wedged on a dusty shelf
behind a rose-pattern, porcelain trinket-tray.
A souvenir of occupied Japan,
the Hakata doll's bisque colors had grayed,
the facial expression still intent on a fish
spread below its upraised hand,
the grip empty of the cleaver it once held.

At home, each clay doll carries its value
in what it holds dear: a lantern,
spear, or story stick.

The next day, I washed dishes under
the garden window, watching my husband
watering my vincas, my potato vines.

It's how I described him in a story once.
He tips the handle—a virtuoso with the spout—
following up with what I've planted.

If I sculpted him out of clay, I'd plant
a fixed watering can in his broad hand.
I'd call the piece *Marriage Doll: 1 of 2*.

—Luanne Castle

Puppet World

for Peter Balkwill's Puppet Intensive Workshop

Beauty is not
what they want, the puppeteers,
pummeling the gray clay into lumps,
shaping a seal, a toothless crone,
grimacing gargoyle, blind old man,
dog face, wolf face, warty moon—
sculpted, scraped, punched and pasted,
lips plumped up, eyes punched in,
hair wire-brushed, frown lines grooved—
from here they'll cast the heads in plaster,
wait a day to dry the molds, dig out
their work, pour in liquid slip, let it
briefly harden, pour off the residue
like a runny omelet on a skillet,
peel out a mask that celebrates
every screw-up of concentration,
slip of hand, air-bubbled nostril
and misaligned chin to reveal
Selkie, Cerberus, Coyote, Clown.

On stage they abandon speech
for squeaks and grunts and spurn
a narrative for surreal leaps and bumps
and jettison props for a plain black cloth
and project their inner demons
into a strutting tin can man,
a feather duster flirt,
a stiff stuffed pillow of a wife,
a lusty humping dog,
an irresistible bottle

tipped to the drunkard's mouth—
character revealed
in each brief move.

For this they've practiced weeks
of being in their bodies,
yoga daily, deliberate walking,
eyes almost closed, feeling the space
around them disclose the other,
carrying their puppet souls.
Awareness stretched
into the other—and we follow
where it goes; don't see
three people standing there
moving a puppet's head
and hands, but his head bending
thoughtfully to read
the pages of a newspaper
that he turns. We can almost
see the words.

—*Robin Chapman*

On the Work Ethic

It's not so much that you subscribe to it
as that you were enlisted in its rolls
from birth and knew you must find work and do it
as soon as you had finished playing dolls
(although you still think wistfully of the one
with true blue eyes and thick, black eyelashes
who'd wet her gown and cry until the moon
turned off its light and left the window sashes
to shiver through a night of wind and snow.
Your doll was fast asleep now, dreaming of
places she'd like, when she grew up, to go
in Santa's merry sleigh, which had paused on the roof
of this shabby tenement long enough to leave
you the Christmas gift of a child to love.)

—Kelly Cherry

The Secret Lives of Little Girls

How loudly you can groan if you just use your eyes.
Children are adept at this, twelve-year-old girls especially.
Alone, high in mountain caves along cliffsides
accessible solely by toeholds and birds of prey,
they deflate and slouch a bit in ease.
At such times they might play jacks or jump a rope,
its woven line slapping the cave roof, freeing
gypsum flowers to flutter down in fragments
over reeking hides and doll parts piled in corners,
a sleeping area of matted glossy magazines,
a fire ring of rolled socks in particolored balls,
simple flint implements, a clamshell for stripping pelts,
small animal bones for holding a bow in the hair,
a pompom here and there caked with glitter and mud.
Hidden in the back beyond reach of firelight, a dollhouse—
perfectly split down the center as eggs rarely are—
where the gods live. The mommy god and the daddy god
stand facing each other either side of a four-poster bed,
a cellophane fire in the living room hearth below.
A dining room table set for three, three plates, three napkins,
and cutlery—a clear plastic goblet at each place.
In the daughter chair, an acorn balanced atop an acorn.
A smile scraped into the top one,
presumably by sharpened antler bone.

—Christopher Citro

Doll Suitcase

Little empire of Barbie,
rectangular, snug, safe,
with a white plastic handle
and tiny lock, before lovers
or husbands opened it
into rapturous disorder.

This was longing, girlish,
doe-like, for forget-me-nots
and trelliswork, a satin gown
in ice blue, bell-skirted
with shoes dyed to match,
a first kiss wreathed
in significance at twilight.

Our desire, quiet and cool,
hung there on plastic hangers
like the tiny clothes, puffed,
frilled, perpetually adrift.
The red plunge neckline dress
floated. Its white tulle skirt
flared from a bodice dotted
with red hearts that interrupted
a chaste white sea of skirt.

Hearts lived there, red
as the boy's flushed face,
bed as the scratchy bricks
behind my shoulders as he
pushed me against a porch wall

staining satin, crushing his boutonniere
of pale chrysanthemums.

Then the hoarse sobs, the fumbling
words we gave away,
took back, gave.

—Geraldine Connolly

The Pregnant Doll

at the Victoria and Albert Museum of Childhood, London

Never an ultrasound's shadowed green, slush and slur of heartbeat,

her plastic body is only visible if you remove
her mother's stomach the size and color of a vanilla wafer,

stomach sliding off neatly to extract the baby, baby
like a battery snapped into the back of a digital clock.

Baby who never cries. Doll who wears heels and a pink nightie
over her emptiness. She's thin in an instant. Never

an IV's bite and scrawl, never a monitor black-strapped on her skin,
never an injection into the cervix that doesn't work. Her body

opens easily, with a finger flick, then closes. She's never
birthsick or tired of being a household for another body.

She's never a cut steak leaking blood onto a plate.

—*Nicole Cooley*

Because a Matryoshka Doll Is a Nest Made of Eggs

At least she is safe. At least
her body of wood rounds at bottom.
And if she breaks, as she must, thrust
into hands happiest if they hurt her,
if she splits or shatters or goes fine, at least
she grows smaller and smaller with each dose
of the other's pleasure, as sparrows narrow their
numbed bodies to burrow into holes carved
from cold. And if she is all hole, opening always
as sky opens to take in the wound of snow, at least—
cut her paint of patterned petals six times, she holds,
at core, a kernel of girl, a seed of soul, her once-
smile now a pin-O, voiceless, snugly screaming.

—*Gillian Cummings*

The Doll Maker

She pours their faces, porcelain
legs and arms resting on every surface:
kitchen counter, night stand, her belly.
She sews cloth bodies. Assembles them
outside her womb—
these hundred virgin doll births.

As she affixes the appendages, soft
white torsos accept their shape, floppy
body now an asterisk, a naked star.
The doll maker is thrifty, sewing
patchwork clothing from old sheets
or her own worn-out dresses.
Waits for her thick hair to grow
long enough, lifts the sharp
edge of sheers,
collecting every strand.

Her steady hand invents
each face: a peach kiss to the lips,
the cheeks—a breeze of pink.
When she finishes, they line her bed
while she speaks a name into each
closed ear. *Sarah*, she whispers
to the smallest and thinks
she has her mother's throat.

—Laura E. Davis

Frozen Charlotte

> *A Frozen Charlotte was a popular 19th-century doll that recalled several ballads about a young woman who froze to death on the way to a county ball.*

I am a doll of ivory bisque.
I was a girl, but was too bold.
To preen in silks, I dared to risk
the open sleigh. I don't grow old.

A girl of flesh who died of cold.
I froze while riding to the ball,
to end in ice and snowy pearls.
I thawed in kilns, a molded doll,

a pocket vanitas for girls.
My cheeks are flushed. I died of cold.
I float now in a child's bath,
my little mistress pushes me

from rim to rim, or to her mouth.
They've taken all my finery.
A doll's not flesh. I don't get cold.
I'm safe for play—no moving parts.

My price is small. I'm bought and sold.
I fortify their frozen hearts.
I'm warmer now—the story's told
on mountain roads. I died of cold.

—Susan de Sola

The Golem

I understand the magic of dead things,
the resurrection of mud into matter,
desiring, as I do, to recreate you from clay,
dry grass, beach glass and sand,
wood shavings, graphite, the earth
around your plain pine box. Anything,
to bring you back. Some seed
or pod. Some breeze to breathe
life into you.

I would sit beside you. Breathless,
we would drive away. In our silence
I might forget Golem do not speak,
cannot differentiate the living
from the dead and out of ignorance
do harm. No one in this room
has risen from the dead. No one's
kiss tastes of maggots and ash,

but nothing would stop me
from blending my mortar
of grief and desire to will
you here. I am ready to die.
I would follow you anywhere.

—Jessica de Koninck

The Room at the House in Croton

Stucco walls to trace small fingers over,
lacy bedclothes, white sheets
smelling of bleach and sweat,
maple furniture with pink knobs,
drawers brimming with sun-dried clothing,
fresh from the line, then starched
with spray on Mother's ironing board.

Shaped like a piano,
music box opened,
played Brahms' lullaby.
A ballerina turned on red felt,
folded down when closed.
Record player in the corner
scratched out thirty-threes.
My brother and I danced
on oak floors.

Treasure chest overflowing
with dress-up clothes.
We were princess and cowboy,
china tea set, beaded necklaces and dolls.
Porcelain faces with shiny blue eyes
that opened and closed, with lashes,
their dresses and tiny black shoes with
straps littering the round white rug.

Little brother, fresh from his bath,
wrapped in white terry towel
dragged through my neatly
arranged tea party, tipping
Chatty Kathy, making her moan,

teddy bears rolling around on the
floor—running from me, trailing
wet footprints out the door.

—Lori Desrosiers

The Doll Museum

The stone dolls, found in an Egyptian tomb,
are eyeless, armless, heavy for a child

to hold. Not like the dolls that lined the room
my sister and I shared, their bodies light

and made for being bent, their eyelids mobile,
hair that tangled with our own at night.

And while we were asleep they came to life.
We never pressed our cheeks against cold stone

as pharaoh's daughters did. The doctor's knife
could not have caught my sister more off-guard

or left me less alone; I had my dolls.
Though, soon, they lay on tables in the yard

with price tags. Even then they looked alive,
survivors with no sickness to survive.

—Caitlyn Doyle

Florida Doll Sonnet

I love Fresh Market but always feel underdressed
squeezing overpriced limes. Louis Vuitton,
Gucci, Fiorucci, and all the ancient East Coast girls
with their scarecrow limbs and Joker grins.
Their silver fox husbands, rosy from tanning beds,
steady their ladies who shuffle along in Miu Miu's
(not muumuus) and make me hide behind towers
of handmade soaps and white pistachios. Who
knew I'd still feel like the high school fat girl
some thirty-odd years later? My Birkenstocks
and my propensity for fig newtons? Still, whenever
I'm face to face with a face that is no more real
than a doll's, I try to love my crinkles, my saggy
chin skin. My body organic, with no preservatives.

—Denise Duhamel and *Maureen Seaton*

In the Milk House

after the town swelled
swallowed the farms in its path
the abandoned milk house
dark but for one small window
sat solid   useless
at the end of our gravel drive

I moved in   I was six
apple crate cupboard   terry towel on the window
rag rug to cover the cold cement
wicker basket for my doll

for a different child this shelter might have been
a clubhouse   a place to hide   to brood
for me a nest where
if I stood on tiptoe at the window
I could watch the gardener next door
tend to her young

I gathered chickweed and dandelion
to nourish my babe
I swaddled   sang   soothed
until each blue eye closed
with a tiny click

I was not neighborly
no imaginary husband
clattered about   I was content
alone with my child

still on occasion
a visitor knocked   stooped to enter
a different mother

one who thought I should know
my baby would melt if
I left her too long in the sun.

—*Jane Ebihara*

Colleen Moore's Doll House

Museum of Science and Industry, Chicago, Illinois

Inside us sits the perfect house.   Lights burn.   Milk flows.
A mother and a father love us and each other,
                            tuck us into warm beds.

The attic slants to shadow, hiding heirlooms. Basement treasures
smack of lavender sachet and ink:

        satin wedding dresses wrapped in tissue,
        lost tribes mapped in 1950's National Geographics.

So it was not the German U-boat,
not fetuses in jars,
not the coal mine's perfect night,
not the octopus suspended from the ceiling,
and not the gaudy walk-through heart
I fell for,

        but a silent movie star's doll house,
        filling a museum room at child height.

Field-trip voyeurs, peering through its incandescent windows,
we circled
        tables set with thumbnail-sized Royal Doulton china,

        chandeliers that pulsed and winked with current,

        streams of water spitting
                from the silver-spigot mouths of dolphins,

        a bedspread made of golden spider web,

        thousand-year-old Chinese vases small as thimbles,

        the smallest slippers ever made, one-quarter-inch long,
                crimson felt with hand-sewn leather soles,

       seahorses and sea snails
              holding up the shells of furniture.

Scattered through the rooms, tiny books, some first-editions,
some handwritten, older than a century.

       On the left prie-dieu, a tiny Bible,
           on the right, *Lives of the Saints*.

       A dictionary, locket-sized, printed with letters A to Z.
         Given by her father, he told her
              she would find inside all the words
                    to make life riveting.

In my house, *Reader's Digest*, *Photoplay,* and *Star,*

      no penciled portrait in a silver frame,
      no central heat,

      but an oil stove sputtered out by morning,
      chilly bedrooms,
      and the bathroom floor, an icy maze
          of white ceramic hexagons
               never warming quick enough.

Leaning in to see that castle, my eyes
      occult as oil-smudged isinglass,
my cheeks flushed with dreams
         as impossible as the three bears'
             chairs seated on a pinhead,

I yearned, not for the priceless objects,
but for the perfect life
        I was certain burned inside that house.

Steadied by imagination, I climbed the floating staircase
with no handrails, already learning how

the hinged heart,
        trap door to every treasure,

only opens with the word.

—Susan Elbe

How to Hold on to the Magic of Fathers

If it is a small Connecticut town in the forties
and he sells, perhaps for Colliers, traveling
all week through the Northeast Kingdom,
clamp down your heart and turn ordinary.

Be good, so good that you might undo
the sighs of your mother as she bends
close to the tabletop Philco
as if trying to hang on
to the last theme note of "Just Plain Bill."
So well-behaved that when your brother
smothers a chick in the bureau
or runs away to the pond,
she will braid your hair and tell you
how very good you are.

And be patient, because sooner or later
it will be a weekend or Christmas. It will be night
and you, dreaming. Having learned to expect nothing,
you'll wake up astonished at the sudden movement
of cold air, its hint of whiskey, the damp
woolly smell of an overcoat. When you feel

his black mustache scraping your cheek,
hold your breath. Light will swell from the bedroom lamp,
your heart pump so largely against your chest
that walls and ceiling will dance.
And when the doll he's carried for miles
appears from beneath his coat, shimmering
in blue taffeta, you'll conjure a name,
let's say Susan or Rachel or Princess,
and hold out your arms to him.

—Patricia Fargnoli

Metal Doll

Madwoman, rooting
through our garbage for those
perfectly good stockings with runs in them.

Mom, come back into the house,
I begged, regretting the rage
I had unleashed.

Years ago, you gave me
your tiny Mexican amulet—
brass mask of an Aztec god

two hollow bells
suspended from his ears,
his grin confirming

fear's great power.
Now you have been boxed up
and carted away.

Yesterday I finished making
a metal doll, laboring
to snip the thick sides

of a can of Bulgarian Feta
inches at a time. Edges
drew blood when carelessly brushed.

Who is this can injure me so easily?
Arms, legs fastened with grommets
so she can dance, neck, waist

riveted stiff. Torso
made from a tin
of Danish butter cookies,

breastplate of pictures from my favorite
Hans Christian Andersen tale—
The Ugly Duckling.

Arms akimbo on her hips, she wears
gold washers for bracelets, an anklet
of blue and white glass beads.

My heart pounds
as I hang your rhinestone flower earrings
from her large ears.

Her skirt jingles—your copper bracelet
of pre-war European coins
darkened with age. Finally, reluctantly,

I fasten the grinning mask around her neck.
Fully dressed, terrifying,
you've returned to be worshipped once again.

—Roberta Feins

The Rat Doll

You're a plump one, rat, your belly's full of blood
and the greasy feathers of ravens.
A bobolink beats its wings inside your ribcage.
In your greed you've swallowed needles and floss,
the tangled manes of horses—then gulped
the pebbled stars, washed down the moon.
And now you turn on the woman who stitched you,
the woman who gave you heft and shape.
Such peace, you snarl, when you've polished off
the cosmos—King of the ripe dominions,
wipe your whiskers in the dust. Wriggle your
felty ears and pull your inky cloak around you.
Get ready to dance. Pull on your scrabbly shoes.

—Ann Fisher-Wirth

Snake Ladies

Then rising from the bathtub we wrapped ourselves in towels and began to dance the Dance of the Snake Ladies in that steamy, shadowy room, clutching our towels but weaving our hips in the nine-year-old version of sinuous circles, jerking our heads from side to side, oh we were transfixed by what we thought was evil, and slithering into the hall, into my little sister's bedroom where she was playing jacks with my Snake Lady partner's little sister, we coaxed them into our dance. Soon they in their nightgowns and we in our towels were bumping and grinding and dipping and weaving, then my Snake Lady partner's towel fell off and soon we were naked, all four, chubby bellies and hairless fronthinds, as we called them, we turned off the lights and my Snake Lady partner whispered *Let's play mommy* so we slithered to the toy shelves and chose four animals, mine was my teddy bear Fuzzy, my little sister's was her bear Kathy, our friends had Tigger and Roo, and writhing in the darkness, we held them to our nipples.

—Ann Fisher-Wirth

Dolls for Sale

How arbitrary the placement
of the dolls in the toy store:
Some in the dark, nestled
in popcorn packaging
listening to the hum
of the furnace and the clip
clopping of the clerks. Some
on display in the front
at the mercy of grimy digits,
fierce, unprovoked hugs and
the ogling, the clamoring,
the disappointment
upon further inspection.
The majority on the top shelf,
waiting with the dust and
the moths, the accumulated
weight of secret debris,
the disintegration of the paint
and pinafores, the movement
towards grime.
The cast-offs on clearance:
relegated to the back rack
with the other $1 specials.
The broken race cars,
the mismatched Legos,
the ones that have been
mishandled, neglected
or thrown.

—*Kelly Fordon*

I Go Back to the Doll Hospital

After two nights of research, I swallow the pills
not licensed for pregnancy, having decided
to believe the doctor when she says
it's the only way to keep my daughter alive.

I made this choice once as a child
when sending my favorite doll into experimental
transplant surgery: my best friend biting
her lip before pulling one leg off
and trying to replace it with another.

How could we have known the new leg
would never work, its bend no longer
a bend but a snap as it swiftly fell to the floor.

I think now of my friend's face as she tried
all afternoon to connect leg with hip,
her eyes refusing to meet mine.

We thought if we fixed what we could see
the dolls would be happier, the dresses
and shoes easier to slip on—no more
trips to the hospital or casts fashioned
from the last tissues in the box.

—Kerri French

The Doll

for Betsy

1.

Cloth body. Wooden head
with painted marcelled hair
and painted eyes. Blink
and they were brown.
Like me she was—brown hair
brown eyes—but better. White
dimity frock with pink rosette.
Rosy knees and socks of lace.
Sister named her *Ugly. Her eyes
wider than her mouth. Miss Ugly.*
Her mouth wore dimples. Pursed.
I was five. I knew her worth.

Mama Mama she used to weep
when I'd lay us down to sleep
pray to God my soul to keep
and if I die before I wake
               and when I woke
and sat her up—brown hair and eyes.
Same body, same white dress
with pink rosette. Same smell.

I'd feed her with a dolly spoon,
touch her lips, count one two three
then eat the food myself.
Sister laughed. Mother hid her face.
What mystery is transubstantiation
when you are five? I knew love.
I understood.
               Then around her mouth
a hurt, a sore that wouldn't heal.
That is, the paint around her mouth—
an ugly sore that spread. Fixed

was all I wanted. A dab of paint.
How Mother iodined my knee. So what
if she were scarred and wore a mark.
I knew love and understood.

And so I laid me down to sleep,
prayed to God her soul to keep
and if she die before I wake
                      and when I woke—
same body. Same beloved dress.
Same smell. But the head was wrong.
The skin too white.
The hair not brown but black.
And when I sat her up, my baby's eyes
of painted brown flew open—glass
and glittered at me, blue.

2.

The trouble is
I never understood.

Shame on you. Look how bad
you made your father feel
who went out of his way
to take a doll to a real hospital
just to make you happy. And look.
She has blue eyes, blue eyes.
Any other little girl in the world
would be thrilled with blue eyes
instead of brown instead of brown
and a new head a new head a new head.

How dare I not be happy
when so much depended on it?

3.

Next scene: flip the pages
of fifty-eight more years.
See my father—Mister Blunder
the mess-up kid—dead
in a hospice room. My father
who used to wash his face
with such a smack and joyful noise
then slick his auburn hair.

Whose head is this—
this bald and toothless wonder?
I examine the neck for transplant,
the line of the old switcheroo.
And I think, maybe if I search
I could find his other head—
his Daddy head—the way years later
I found my doll's in a grocery sack
back of Mother's closet. But then
where to store this one?
In what closet? what paper bag?

Old-man doll on a pillow,
clutching in an icy fist your last
dim handful of heat, your nose
poking up in terror as if you died
smelling your last breath coming, tell me.

—*Alice Friman*

Doll Heads

Doll heads are washing up on the beach.
They are bald, the bald heads of little babies
neatly severed from their torsos.

Did you, as a child, ever light a doll on fire?
Back in those days, dolls would burst into flame,
practically explode. There was a fuse-like

searing sound, and a smell, do you
remember the smell? Burning manikins
smell that way too, like glass burning.

Doll heads are discovered in trees.
No one was seen placing them in the branches.

Doll heads can be found under pillows
and inside of small boxes. It has been surmised
that a person's head remains conscious

for one minute after decapitation.
I don't know, you'd have to ask the head.
If it is conscious, can it speak?

Insurgents have been beheading our people.
Barbaric you say? Yes, I suppose so,
a kind of low-budget shock and awe.

A bomb crashes in on a restaurant.
Oops, our target was not there tonight.

The customers stand and dust off their clothes.
Some of the food is still edible.
Now the restaurant is outdoors.

Doll heads are drifting in with the tide.
Their little pates bobbing in the waves,
rolling a bit, coming to rest, some sideways

on one cheek, some face down, a few,
the lucky ones, looking up at the clouds.

—Richard Garcia

What the Children Know

The mothers seem already
to have forgotten.

Dolls emerge from tissue
and the mothers admire
the honey-thick hair, lash-lined
china eyes, the crisp dresses.

What the mothers have forgotten
children know unfailingly.

Children croon
to the frozen faces, their own
inverted in the aggie eyes.

Vinyl shoes and small dresses
are left to closets or the underworld
of beds. Dynel hair
knots and features grime while
the children and the blank-trunked
dolls rehearse their
lock-kneed goosestep.

Dolls serenely ride
the dump trucks, aeroplanes,
or roller skates straight
into tragic accidents.

Pale eyes roll shut
in their heads as they fall.

No matter.

In the night those eyes
click open wide. Smiling

their paralyzed smiles,
dolls leave the shelves, the beds.

Deep in the darkness
each knows exactly
how to find us.

—Christine Gelineau

Pretty Baby

The photo shows me in navy shorts and white blouse,
camp uniform for visiting day. Mama snapped
me next to the large field where an archery range
stood when parents weren't there.

Next to the field—a tool shed. *Campers Forbidden*,
the sign said. Back home again, shocking news:
Bruce L found inside, abdomen cut open, a wayward
axe planted by his head.

But that August day, Plymouths and Pontiacs crunched
across the gravel parking lot. Bruce, lanky and tan,
still alive, our parents visiting with salamis and rye
for bunkmates to share, to temper tears after dark.

I posed for the Kodak Brownie, my arms around
Sparkle Plenty, that year's doll rage. Sparkle Plenty,
fifteen inches high, blonde hair down her back,
first doll ever with *magic skin* that darkened with age.

Who could have guessed that such a beauty would be born
to Gravel Gertie and her equally ugly husband B.O. Plenty?
Sparkle Plenty, every girl's dream doll, my dream doll,
brought to camp that day.

Where did she go, my Sparkle Plenty? I've searched for
her at train and toy meets, always told, *None here*.
Sparkle Plenty, star that brightened the Sunday funnies,
that lit up a child's sky before darkness came for Bruce.

—*Gail Fishman Gerwin*

My Mother's Doll

Perched in her antique carriage, she watches
all through glassy eyes, a cloudy blue much like
my mother's eyes, now nearly useless.

A head of sculpted bisque nestled in a
bonnet turning yellow. We have no plans for her.

She's part of Mother's legacy of porcelain,
like the cupboard stacked with gold-rimmed plates
for dinners in the afterlife. Delicate accumulations

turned to lead, the crystal goblets' patterns cut
with heft to prove that beauty can be sustenance
but has a weight to bear.

Here, in glass-front cabinets, beside the
table of no-meals—a worn mahogany, listing
on its broken pedestal—everything

waits for what never happens. The table
is set. Toys look down from the attic. The doll
makes her proclamation, eyes wide

in perpetual startle:
you will never have children.

—Meredith Davies Hadaway

Unfound Love Note

In Boulder Creek, a blow-up doll folds her flat
limbs in on herself and stares at the sky. She'd

jumped in after her heart, but it was only
a floating aspen leaf, red in late September.

The last time she thought she found her heart,
it was a Braeburn apple on the sidewalk, fallen

from a hand or a grocery bag, its blush unblemished
but for a tiny black heart—a heart on a heart!—

a surprise on the shadowy underside,
like a scar or a tattoo you only show your lover.

Nobody told her it would take her whole,
satisfaction-guaranteed life to find something

blood-warm and pulsing
inside her soft, plastic chest.

—Marj Hahne

Operation Teddy Bear

It must all be done in secret,
late at night, the prized object
pried from the arms that clutch it in sleep.
For months you've noticed how abject

he looks, sitting on the sofa
with his head resting on his hips,
his torso shrunken to nothing,
as if love were a kind of hardship

leading to physical starvation.
His fur too looks diseased,
worn away in patches. But nothing
can be done about these—

nor about his eyes, clouded and cracked
as if from glaucoma or cataracts.
Don't look into them now or
you may lose your resolve to act.

Instead, turn the animal face down
on the kitchen counter and try
to think of yourself as a surgeon,
and not of how your child would cry

and scream to see what happens next:
his father slitting the bear's neck
with the scalpel of an X-Acto blade.
Now there is no turning back.

Hurriedly, as if you might be caught,
you cram the new stuffing in
like a smuggler hiding drugs,
then stitch up the wound again.

Nothing lasts is a notion
your child can't grasp. In the morning
he'll find his bear robust again
but with a scar like a warning.

—Jeffrey Harrison

Bad Times Barbie

Things hadn't been *really* good for Barbie and Ken for a long time, but Barbie had managed to keep up appearances, her chin up, her upper lip stiff. First, there was the affair with Midge while Barbie was having her boobs re-done. Then Ken began showing more than a brotherly interest in Skipper. He spent a lot of time at the track and in Vegas, always dropping a bundle. He blamed all his *little problems* on drinking and his drinking he blamed on Barbie. Still, Ken was financially successful, so Barbie took him back time and time again. Then crash! The savings and loan scam! Ken was a player. What with the legal fees and the time behind bars, the camper had to go, then the Vette, and finally the place in Malibu. Barbie hated the way the jailhouse coveralls brought out the yellow in Ken's complexion, so she started seeing G.I. Joe. Joe had been hot for Barbie since high school, but being from the wrong side of the tracks and clearly not going anywhere, hadn't stood a chance. Joe figured he had Barbie over a barrel, so he moved her and what was left of her accessories down to Orange County near his work at El Toro. But, with the talk of base closings, the stress was too much for him. He went on a bender and flashed back to Nam. He roughed Barbie up, pulling out hair, denting a breast. Meanwhile, Ken gets out of prison and joins the men's movement. He goes looking for a father with his new accessories: poems and a set of drums. Now, Barbie hangs out at the Orange County Swap Meet, selling off the rest of her stuff along with the puffy-paint t-shirts she's learned how to make. In bad times, Barbie figures, to be flexible *is* best.

—Donna Hilbert

Carriage

I had my own baby carriage
for my baby dolls to ride in
a fine, four-wheel thing
with padded handlebar and springs
mattress and folding canopy

to hide my babies from the sun
or unwanted, jealous glares
they rode in royal high style

I don't remember the dolls within
but that my father would carry me
the pram and brown bags of groceries
in his strong, strong arms up five flights
of steep stairs

—Akua Lezli Hope

Plié

My aunt's bedroom was a place
I was rarely allowed
with its lace and bows, dancers
embroidered on pillow cases,
the doll on the bed, crocheted
ruffles spilling from her waist.
Even the dressing table,
fancy and curved, the candy pink
skirt was delicate and sweet.
The girl under the silver dome
was always on her toes,
arms circled, pink tutu rippling,
as she twirled to "Für Elise."
I wanted to touch her
fingers, so delicate they might
break. But there was no touching
at my grandmother's house
and every time I asked, my aunt
covered the music box while the girl
bowed and folded inside herself.

—Karla Huston

Alan Doll Rap

When I was ten
I wanted a Ken
to marry Barbie
I was into patriarchy
for plastic dolls
eleven inches tall
cuz the sixties hadn't yet
happened at all
Those demonstrations
assassinations
conflagrations across the nation
still nothin but a speck in the imagination
Yeah, Ken was the man
but my mama had the cash
and the boy doll she bought me
was ersatz
"Alan" was his name
from the discount store
He cost a dollar ninety-nine
Ken was two dollars more
Alan's hair was felt
stuck on with cheap glue
like the top of a pool table
scuffed up by cues
and it fell out in patches
when he was brand new
Ken's hair was plastic
molded in waves
coated with paint
no Ken bad-hair days
Well they wore the same size
they wore the same clothes
but Ken was a player
and Alan was a boze
Barbie looked around
at all the other Barbies

drivin up in Dream Cars
at the Ken-and-Barbie party
and knew life had dealt her
a jack, not a king
knew if Alan bought her
an engagement ring
it wouldn't scratch glass
bet your ass
no class
made of cubic zirconia
or cubic Plexiglas
Kens would move Barbies
out of their townhouses
into their dream-houses
Pepto-Bismol pink
from the rugs to the sink
wrap her in mink
but Alan was a bum
Our doll was not dumb
She knew a fronter from a chum
Take off that tuxedo
Alan would torpedo
for the Barcalounger
Bye-bye libido
Hello VCR
No job, no car
Drinkin up her home bar
Stinkin up her boudoir with his cigar
Shrinkin up the cash advance
on her MasterCard
and tryin on her pink peignoir
Till she'd be saying:
"Where's that giant hand
used to make him *stand,*
used to make him *walk*?"

—Julie Kane

Cloth Doll with Found Feathers

after a sculpture by Lisa Culjis Macdonald

She's tacked,
hemmed, mended
and since, like us, she hides
her past, her back is
sutured, the twisted
knots looped tight
as koans or sutras.

A totem for midlife?

Gravity pitches her
splayed limbs akimbo;
her cloth so thinned
we see clear through
to the eggshell ghost
of stuffing underneath.

Her smile is mystical:
realistic but tidy.
Her winter berries
are wired on, like her hoop
of crow and pigeon
feathers, palm frond skirt.

(Before birth, in an alternate
life, her body was
scraps; she polished cloudy
bureaus, buffed them up,
then retired, anonymous
and calm.)

Softness extrudes
but holds her
steady. Pliability
erects her.

—Susan Kelly-DeWitt

Ginny

All my friends had Ginny dolls with more dresses
than I had. *My* Ginny arrived in November for my seventh
birthday. I hoped Santa would bring her clothes
and furniture like my girlfriends had for their Ginnys.

What I found under the tree was Ginny-sized furniture
my father made, long nights while I slept, crafted from pine
and upholstered—not *real* Ginny furniture, but pieces that
matched what my parents had when they were first married.

Years later, after my parents were gone, I found Ginny
and her furniture in the cellar of our old house, carefully
packed with a note in my mother's handwriting: *I thought
you might want these someday*. I brought them here to *this*
house, recovered the sofa and chair, restored Ginny's red hair.

Ginny lives in my bedroom now, in a glass case
with the furniture my father made. Sometimes, I wish
I lived there too, looking through glass from the inside out.
I'd curl into Ginny's chair, sleep on her sofa.
I'd talk to her about the perfection of shadows.

—Adele Kenny

The Way It Broke

Rapid fire, heartbeat
pulsates head to toe
as passion once imperishable
tumbles down the stairs,
a shattered doll.

Shards of porcelain
prickle, poke, pierce
clammy skin—
their marriage
scattered on the floor.

—Laurie Kolp

Scary Movie

There's always an old house,
clapboard or stone—
it doesn't really matter which
as long as it appears at the end of a path
that winds all the way
to the heart of fear's labyrinth.
If there's a dollhouse, even better.
Let its owner peer through the windows
and see herself in miniature,
her life reclining safe
on the surface of childhood.
Let her not remember yet
how night's bony finger
used to tap out a summons
from inside its coffin.

Instead, instruct her to open
the tiny music box
no bigger than a fingertip.
Note the way its tune
haunts her sanity
in predictable increments
until there's nothing left of her mind
but the ghosts whose voices
ring out across reason.
But know, too, that in this
version of suffering she will always
find the staircase curving away from terror—
that before the credits roll
she'll unlock the past's rusted door,
and stumble back into happiness.

—Lori Lamothe

Behind the Glass

When I have driven myself again into the wall of my own free will,
I want to go back to childhood, to be a small statue in porcelain,
to be all ringlets and eyelashes,
to be flawless and empty of lust.

Make me a doll like this—
curl my mouse brown hair, spin it gold
and forever untangled,
comb out the knotted lies, or cut them.

Plump my lips in youth and rose them, round my face again. Halt
slow-sliding age, the creeping stop of my living body.
Make me forget the gradual fade of my flowers.
Edge me in lace to yellow with decades; clothe me in satin to thin.

Encircle my lonely waist and stand me up behind display.
Hold me by silver-tone while my toes graze a mahogany stage.
Let me watch over a little girl in her lavender bedroom
and beg her silently with my glass eyes—

to stay away from growing up.

From behind the glass I'll watch her
flaw and pain and smear away her innocence,
and, unless boxed or sold, watch her girl become a woman, too—

and see it over and over, as porcelain behind the glass
smug and unwanting in my edited youth,
incapable of stopping time for anyone other than me.

—*Jessica Wiseman Lawrence*

Paper Doll Ghazal

When she was twelve, she had a shoebox full of tatty dolls
with painted tag board faces—creased and worn-out shabby dolls.

She loved Elizabeth Taylor the most—those violet eyes
and small waist a far cry from her buggy full of chubby dolls.

Kim Novak had a blonde mystique about her quiet face—
but sultry in pajamas—ruffled pink paper baby dolls.

Coquettish Debbie Reynolds smiled the widest of them all.
Why not? She'd hauled in Eddie Fisher—that hunky hubby-doll!

Old Betty Davis must have been a hand-me-down: cousins'
boxes of outgrown clothes sometimes held a grubby doll.

Seasons changed, there was no Bloomingdale's for paper girls—
no mall—the Sears catalog gave hope for all but snobby dolls.

Swimsuits painted on, they couldn't really change. But at thirteen,
Chris donned a bra and a cardboard smile like all unhappy dolls.

—Christina Lovin

Delaware Guardian Doll

Red-paint oak face   ruffled brooched collar
maroon skirt   flounced   red-bead moccasins
black hair   bound bun   oak leaf appliqué:
Delaware Dance doll   two-hundred years old

      Great-grandmother gone
      buried by the north branch creek
Wyandotte County cemetery

I remember my mother's story
      how they rode city trolleys to buy dolls
      as many as she wanted, store-bought

More at home: cornhusk, raggedy anns, clay

      She taught me to belt a hollyhock blossom
how to shape the full red-petal skirt

Still my mother keeps dolls
sets of clothes resewn each year:
blouses of crisp voile   boys' shirts in navy
blonde and black-haired   blinking wide eyes
miniature leather shoes   touching earth

—Denise Low

Bambi

No deer at all, the stuffed animal
I opened the door to when I heard a knock.
Unsteady on long legs, its huge ears
cocked as if waiting to hear its name.
"Bambi!" my mother said behind me, and why
not? I wrapped my arms around his neck
and leaned my cheek against his fuzzy jaw.
Hadn't I cried at his mother's death,
his father's stern injunction to care for himself?
Hadn't I even, at a truck stop parking lot, cursed
hunters with a deer strapped to their car?
Lucky they saw the humor, my father said,
though I could tell he was proud.
And when my neighbor, a boy I didn't trust
because he pulled the wings from locusts, twirled
Bambi by one ear till it broke clean off,
didn't I grab a ruler and thwack him so hard
his arm carried home a stripe red as a scald?

Bambi wasn't a deer, but a donkey,
my mother later confessed, but as close
as my father could find for a girl who needed
a fawn. The real ones I now don't need
are born just past our fence, learn
to keep their distance, but before they learn,
wobble on stilt legs and stare at me in trust.
I hate them, I say, those rats with hooves,
thieves that ate our garden, tulips, and shrubs
before we made a truce with posts and wire.
Though every so often our gazes lock,
their eyes limpid and bright as the black beads
I gazed at with love when the wild
seemed passive as a doll I could coax
to sleep in the crook of my arm.

—Mary Makofske

After Torrential Rain

Rescue rang at the shock
of pink buttocks, leg toed up
axe-handle from the mud bank, one thigh
an eggshell hole
                  please please not headless.
Sweet shape of the leg
kicked into the air at the angle
of my arm pulling her
up from the earth and the eyes
jounced open, pupils
dilated in a gauze
of red sand.

    *

Whether her mottled skin may wash clear,
I cannot tell until
I touch it boldly, bodily.
Rubella. The eyes of a child
at such a time of fever hurt
inside as though the lids were a veil
of red sand.
              Mother's lips tested for fever
upon my forehead
as a paper brush, a gauge,
dry nurse. I wanted the lips to press
as reflex kiss   churr, a taste.

    *

Doll solution: a hospital.
Warehouse shelves stack corrugated
cartons of factory culls. A lost leg's the easiest.
New hair is a snap. Clip away the harpy bird's nest,
replug the holes with hanks of nylon.
Lather the brown spots
feeding on the surface
like ferment on a peeled apple.

The selves slough off—
infant dies into child who dies into
blue puff veins, papery husk.
We speak of angels
who kiss the lifted forehead.

   *

With the smallest finger of my right hand,
I tip doll's eyelids down.
They close like a rolltop desk.

—Charlotte Mandel

Still Lovers

after Elena Dorfman

> —If you've ever dreamed of creating your ideal partner,
> then you have come to the right place.
> —RealDoll.com

From across the yard she looks elegant,
black hair spilling from blanket to grass,

barefoot, one leg casually bent and leaning
against her lover, who is typing at a laptop

by her side. He is not bad looking.
A little old, a little bald. The kind of man

women with teenage children might smile at
in the grocery store, while reaching out

for a loaf of bread. Another man carries
his brown-haired girl like a bride or an invalid

into the bedroom, propping her on pillows,
arranging her hair and limbs. He changes

her clothes into a black slip and stockings, lays
his face next to hers and breathes the perfume

sprayed into her hair. Her blue eyes look up
into his and always say *yes*, her lips forever parted

and eager. When he holds her at night under heated
blankets, the warmth seeping into the fibers

of their skin, does he feel less lonely than before?
Maybe her smooth, silicone touch is more real

than the touch of a woman who could yawn,
pull up the covers, and turn away.

—Jennifer Matteson

Little Doll

I was the live birth after the stillborn
one, crowned to be Mother's little doll. She
called me Princess, dressed me in ruffles,
lace, too prettied up to make fires like other
children in open lots, where they baked corn
and potatoes, slipped salt shakers taken
from their mothers' kitchens. My doll rode
in a carriage, her dress made by Mother
to match mine. Two dolls. My earrings gold,
hair curled and combed, big bow hand-sewn
of the same fabric as my clothes.
Undressed, baby dolls had smooth bodies,
no crevices. I'd be perfect, never play,
an untouched doll, if mother had her way.

—Joan Mazza

Paper Doll

In a plain white slip she'll never outgrow,
she smiles at the prospect of a new pinafore—
smocked bodice, two ruffles on the skirt.
To her, morning is nothing
but a change of clothes. I don't think

she has weighed the possibilities.
Everything she wears hangs unseamed,
reaching around to her dark side:
a perfect fit when she holds still.
Cardboard has its own posture.

If I hold my shoulders back like her,
I'll be a mother's dream.
Let's say I attach the blue dress,
princess style with tiny pearl buttons
down the front. I could add the skimmer

with pink ribbons, though she hates
how it rides her curls, cocked
as if her head were lopsided.
I put words in her mouth, help her
glide across the room to see her best friend

who lives at the foot of my sister's bed.
Still smiling, the two of them are half ready
to shop with their mothers, go to tea,
or get shoved to near nakedness
by the neighborhood boys.

—*Susan Laughter Meyers*

The Doll Handler Tells the Truth about Them

The dolls have nothing to hide.
They covet our show of white light,
our puffs of nicotine breath.
They like to watch us destroy

what we cannot give up.
They say that we are one half
sleeplessness, one half hunger.
Growing up inside a house full

of miniature trees has taught them
to remain stunted, happy, safe.
Each dollhouse door dreams
of a window and an eye looking past it.

Each dollhouse bottle collects
glitter dust, a season's worth of arsenic.
The dolls carve with gentle hands,
so I never take what they have to give.

The loneliest radio in the world
has a belly of static; the dial pokes
through the bone, blisters the finger tips.
I hear the dolls whisper on every frequency.

—Kristine Ong Muslim

Dollhouse

My father comes home with a cardboard box under his arm
that he knifes open, removing metal walls

with tabs that bend to insert into slits until a house
sits on the floor complete with flower boxes

filled with painted petunias, a red door, a chimney
and one side open to reveal a warren of rooms, two stories,

with diminutive furniture, thumbnail pans on a stove,
patches of fabric rugs and a real plastic family of four,

Americans, the father in a grey suit, blond children,
the mother with an apron tied around her waist.

And a new Buick in the garage, garden tools
lined up against the wall, a lawn mower and a drill.

That was the year my mother went away to live
for months in a hospital where I could not go.

I knew where she was
and that she would come back,

but the house seemed scraped hollow,
and in the silence I felt someone listening

who I thought might be God or a fairy small as a pin,
moth-like, flinging her body on the window glass.

—Gail Newman

The Only House in the Neighborhood

The stove doesn't work. The food is painted
on the refrigerator door. No stairs join

the three levels, and the residents flit
between them: colorful, mute birds. Days

pass with the click of a switch and no matter
if Baby bathes with his clothes on, or Mother

in her fitted purple jacket, heeled shoes,
and with her wild silken hair spends a week

face-down on the laundry room floor, or
if when Father goes to work he is really only

waiting behind the sunroom to come back home.
There is a birthday party nearly every day,

no fear of death or failure, no mortgage
to pay, no money at all. And if the tiny pink

phone in the kitchen never rings, and the doors
don't open, and if the family can't bend

their knees to kneel in the warm square of light
on the plastic-wood floor, they still lie

ready for you to set the table, snap the garden
fence back into place, position the pink crib

next to the blue, fix the girl onto her rocking horse,
and let your hand push the thing until it topples.

—Sarah Rose Nordgren

When You Ask Whether I Ever Played with Dolls

It's true—I loved my cousin's Barbies, how we dressed them
    in fig leaves we fashioned ourselves: violets

superglued to rubber bands. Usually, we'd tuck a pair together,
    snug in their makeshift bed, their arched feet

slipping against each other under the covers. No, the busty
    plastic femmes were never the problem:

what I couldn't abide were the stuffed infants, their puffy skin
    sewn from pantyhose, those eyes that winked

mercilessly open and shut with each shift in the center of gravity.
    Worst of all: my sister's Baby Alive, which ate

and shat Cheery Cherry sugar paste, its mindless automatism
    meant to imitate the digestive functions

of a bona fide baby, and perhaps that's what it did, the likeness
    a remarkable effect until its mysterious innards

were baffled by a blockage, a clump of sweetness lodged inside,
    and when my sister lifted Baby for her daily

ministrations, she found maggots spilling from its bowed lips.
    That night, my mother dumped all the dolls

in the pyre of our burn barrel, and though about this dramatic
    moment, my sister recalls only the smell—

melting plastic, scorched gingham—what haunts me is the sound,
    not just the hiss and pop of the flames,

but the hitching sobs of my sister as she wailed into the hollow
between my mother's collarbone and shoulder.

—Jennifer Perrine

Pediophilia

Love of dolls

The week her daughter died, the room her girl
had occupied became a home for dolls.
The first an angel: fearsome, glass-gazed gift
to dull a mother's utter grief; the next
a paint and porcelain she numbly bought
from QVC. It looked like *her*. And now
she sees her small grandchildren grow, and knows
it's good. But they can't guess each small doll dress
arranged by day comes into disarray
by night. They bring her more, naïve. Don't know
she weeps in the overflowing sea of limbs
that manage, year by year, to commandeer
the bed, the floor, and more. An orphanage
of girls. A thousand eyes that cannot shut.

—*Jessica Piazza*

Every Body She Carries

When my friend tells me this loss
will open the way
to all the others in my life,
I think of the way I am drawn
to the Russian nesting doll
in the toy store I pass each day, how I hold
the wooden egg of her body
in my palm, stare
at her black eyes, her sinuous lashes.
She is painted thick
with earth colors--orange, umber,
green, yellow. I twist her until
every body she carries
is revealed,
until I find the smallest one held
in the marrow of her emptiness
like a single, solid
child alone.

—Andrea Potos

Playing Drunks at Age 7

It was my friend's idea, acting like drunks.
We crept into her garage, grabbed
two empty wine bottles from the garbage,
and ran into the woods.

Taking pretend swigs, we swayed and slurred.
I only knew what I'd seen on *Bonanza:*
I grabbed my bottle by its throat and brought
the heavy end down hard on my friend's head.

It didn't shatter like in the TV barroom brawls,
but my friend's shrieks brought my mother running.
She comforted my friend, eyes focused on me, sharp
as the shards of glass I had expected to see.

When my friend returned home from the hospital,
I was waiting to present her with Velvet, the doll
I had long craved for her magically growing hair.
Forgiven, I pretended to admire her human stitches

but could only think about her head,
blond and soft as the doll's, and how it had flowed
red as the wine I had seen at her house that morning,
a half-filled glass sitting beside the toast.

—Kyle Potvin

The Fear of Puppets and the Fear of Beautiful Women

have in common that your tongue is not your own,
is a hand reaching up through your throat,

making your plastic eyes roll a hard eight.
You have to look at whatever the hand wants,

and it wants to make them laugh, the beautiful women,
but not the way they'd laugh at a dog,

which is what you are. You are covered in fur,
the cheap kind, someone decided you should be orange

like a rug from the decade when everyone was blind,
even the beautiful women, who bred with men in sideburns

and embroidered vests, and one of their offspring was you.
You know the word *venustraphobia*.

It is not a tropical spider with delicate green legs.
The fear of beautiful women is different

from the number thirteen or crossing bridges,
though the fear of being bald is sometimes compared to it.

Beautiful women have not confided in you
about dentists, or the dark, or getting on a plane.

The fear of puppets stays in their heads.
You can still tremble unstrung. Open your mouth.

It might be your own words coming through this time.
Pupaphobia: having a fist for a windpipe,

the fist of the one who holds you on his lap.

—*Jendi Reiter*

Potato Head

I've told you where I'm coming from
so you can piece it together:
Mr. Potato Head sessions with

> Mrs. Potato Head arguing over
> the grocery bill, sex, the imminent
> shutoff of the heat. Here in the basement

of grey cement and bare bulbs,
we jabbed plastic spikes deep into Idaho
spuds, added enormous eyes and ears,

> yarmulkes and long beards.
> In the coldness of that house,
> I built an empire of miniature soaps

from budget inns and Howard Johnsons
for Mrs. Potato Head to drown
in dishwater: her cups and plates dripping

> Sweetheart clean. We played and played
> not knowing the lives we were inventing
> were old flimflam landscapes

of too much work for not enough pay.
Though sometimes we'd borrow an orange
from the fruit bowl and give it a small hat,

> toothpick legs, and blue magic
> marker boots. We didn't need maps
> or mirrors to find a way out of the echo

chambers of childhood—just
a vegetable and a fruit repurposed
for two Jewish girls in a basement

trying with spells and with death-
defying stubbornness, so hard
to reshape the afternoon blues.

—Susan Rich

This Child Left

New Year's Day, my black-hooded coat,
we circle the lake:
    two wild geese left behind, one bonded
    to the flightless other, swim past.

This is our last walk of the year
before branches and rails
    turn into thin, black shadows
    of new snow.

Twenty years after an abortion
my mother arranged for me,
    I weep for not knowing:
    Was it a daughter? Was it a son?

Months, now, I've mined the basement
for relics I might heal:
    Ginny Doll, arms fallen
    off dry rubber band joints;

the relentless smile I magic markered
onto my Mickey Mouse.
    I muff my arms inside my sleeves.
    Could I conceive again?

The geese glide from shore to shore,
weaving runes in their wake:
    the separate *V*s they spread;
    and, between them, the *X*.

        —Susanna Rich

The Apothecary Doll

National Museum of Health and Medicine, Washington, DC

Nearly four feet tall, the woman,
           carved from wood,
     painted and waxed,

has bendable joints.
           Beneath the wooden
     nipples

her flesh has been stripped
           to reveal removable organs,
     liver, kidney, colon, all—

painted mauve and ruby and ocher
           and labeled carefully
     in Chinese.

What magic do you hoard, woman,
           what secret lore
     in your ankles and knuckles,

in your jape and joke,
           your vapor?
     The face is calm, eyes

open, but not too wide,
           eyelids giving
     a languorous gaze

that must have reassured
           the clients who came
     to point at where they hurt,

hoping a pill or salve
           the apothecary mixed
     in his wide-mouthed alabaster mortar

could relieve the pains
            in their own chests,
      return them to their days—

like wooden shapes so neatly classed,
           so precisely ordered—
    healed and whole.

—Kim Roberts

Sonnenizio on a Line from Ciardi

Night after night forever the dolls lay stiff,
their jaundiced eyes ride the doldrums of sleep,
their fitful dreams redolent with spite
for the children who dolled them up, matured, then left.
There is no happy ending for stillness, for idols
who've been locked out, evicted from the dollhouse,
and if the naked and headless aren't quite dolly
birds, with dollops of the sinister about them,
they wield their nostalgic power on adolescents,
scare them with flashbacks of too-sweet dolphin kisses.
They strap bandoliers across their uncurved hips,
divine methodology for blackmail with video clips.
Don't send condolences to the waistline-impaired.
The guile of baby dolls cannot be compared.

—*Marybeth Rua-Larsen*

Flip Doll: Red Riding Hood

You won't find legs beneath
this dolly's blue-flecked gingham skirt.
Or feet. No, there's a cast of characters

below, connected at the waist
and rather intimately, wouldn't you agree?

What kind of toy is this to give a girl?
At least it's obvious the thing's
not anatomically correct.

I flip Red on her head, her skirt
turns sober green and fifty years

fly by: it's grandma! with impressive
sagging breasts, grey curls like painted waves
across her brow. She wears a white nightcap.

Pull it down to cover up her wrinkled face,
then turn her over—ho, ho, ho, the wolf.

He wears the nightcap now,
dress buttoned high to hide the apple
in his throat, that tell-tale scrap

of red cape in his mouth, a tongue. Red's
upside down, in darkness, pigtails touching earth.

Still, they got one moral of this story right
(should you decide to play.) There's
no woodsman. You'll have to save yourself.

—Hayden Saunier

The Promise

He promised to bring me a doll.
He is gone all day. I
trust him. I think how the weather
is chill for a doll from Spain.
Maybe she'll be a Russian,
with layers of wool and babushkas
on her shoulders and head.
A print of spring in her skirt.

I sit on the steps waiting.
He said she was three feet tall.
It didn't seem strange. I'd
heard of people seeing Jesus
bigger than that. My others
are small.

And fancy. Blue faille gown
on Marie Antoinette. White tatted
lace. Napped slippers that feel
like the tongue of the dog.

Mother says time for lunch.
Over my soup I imagine him
bustling her through the door.
Her eyes tilt shut as he lays her
down with the evening paper.

All afternoon on the stoop.
Mother brings me a coat.
If he comes home now, he can tell me
she's still on order. If he
brings her soon, she can be
one foot tall.

It grows dark. Shadows sprinkle
my clothes like dirt. Finally

he comes, carrying nothing
but his hands. His face
does not say regret.
I blush.
I follow him in.

—*Enid Shomer*

I Hit My Sister Across the Back with the Speak-n-Spell

Dog-Dog-Dog

the cyborg
stuttered, voice

of a father
cross her porcelain

back lashed
with my loosed

raging. She vowed
to dye her hair

blonde, change
her name to Lauren.

I let my best friend
slap her, let her eat

my entire Easter basket
so she'd get fat.

And she just had to
get my same

Madame Alexander
baby with spy eyes

that shut

when we plonked
our dumb daughters

on block beds
to sleep, bound

in covers

like mummies
didn't she?

—Lauren Goodwin Slaughter

17th Century Ivory Anatomical Model

Cool as a corpse to the touch, eyes low,
she lies on a velvet-lined base, pocket-sized
as a tattered book of hours, as an iPod
whose click-wheel cracked open. Drop her

and she'll ping on glass, a clutter of pings
as her torso tips and spills tight-wound
intestines, placenta, fetus, each a stutter.
Don't ask her to reassure you. You know

better than she how your body bulges,
how your eyes warp and water, your fingers
swell. Sick all the time, you. She already
dead, she can show only where a child fits.

Even a C-section won't expose you
the way she lifts away; she knows this
and her anemic arm swivels
from her heart to cover her face.

The other hand covers her V, formed
where stiff open legs meet. Gentlemen could
lift that hand, but their curiosity
was for her polished, toy-like exposure.

—Emma Sovich

When Catholics Believed in Limbo

I don't recall if it was holy water
and if so,
would it be a sacrilege

to baptize the rubber dolls
named Amy and Beth,
making the sign of the cross with our palms,

in the name of the Father,
Son,
and back then, the Holy Ghost,

on the bald foreheads with painted rivulets
of hair we christened,
water pouring slowly from a cup,

giving protection from Limbo,
that we believed in then
with such certitude

that even for our dolls
we would not risk
denying entrance into heaven.

—Mary Ellen Talley

Secrets

Somewhere fingernails are being
clipped, staccato, not at all equal.
You can hear this but not the growth
of them in the first place, or of hair.
The oven stays shut and mouths
aren't meant to open. Parts of dolls
are soiled or worn where human
children press, the way anything in the world
that happens leaves a mark. The dolls
are always being picked up and placed
by forces outside their control.
Words are put into their mouths.

—Elaine Terranova

Broken Doll

The moon-feeders are out
and dreams, too, those small moths of the heart.
In the back of beyond
where memory is flawed and flung,
a broken doll lies by the pond,
she—the lost link between yesterday
and tomorrow. Her eyes are missing,
her fingers crimped.
So hurry, child . . .
pull on your boots,
then find and rescue her
before morning comes with
its wafer of winter sunlight.

—Susan Terris

How Dolls Are Made

At 18, partly-formed, confident
in the possibility of my own perfection,
I was drawn by a machine hum
down a narrow street to that doorway:
boxes of heads, bins of torsos,
and the night shift factory workers,
all men, silent, who sliced away
the excess plastic from the bodies
like bargain-basement doctors busy at
liposuction. I watch the tiny figure
of myself watch, in fascination, men
who didn't know they spoke to me
carving arms still warm from molds
with stubby knives, flinging heads streaming
Rapunzel-like hair into cardboard turrets.
I see my glassy eyes open and close,
then blink back real tears.
I see myself shrink back, and back
to my first doll, a hug of rubber
consolation against some childhood sorrow,
recalling at that threshold
the first sense of self in pieces,
a girl-child to be assembled
and shaped by many hands.

—*Maria Terrone*

American Girl

Two ponytails bobbing off the train,
one real-sized head; next to it,
a smaller one, the same
ribbon, the same chestnut hair,
the same brown eyes,
bowed lips—a doll just like her!

Beside them is the mother,
her bob, too, is the color of the hair
of the doll with which she has endowed
her daughter, in glut of love, delivering
another like her, so daughter can,
like a mother, love her
and thereby know herself beloved;
to be trained by this relationship for others,
and someday to discover an other
like a self—to have
and be beloved and lover.

Mini-me, little twin, idealized simulacrum;
might it not also show where one falls short
(a slightly crooked smile, a paler cheek)
or, past the first surprise of recognition
does one cease to see, and love not sight
but something other, essence,
or receptor, that pulls
all that multitude of tender feelings
with which girls are often full to surfeit?

The three shining heads pass me
haloed under station's pale fluorescents
in triangulate devotion, they climb the stairs
love-girdled, sufficient.

—*Marjorie Tesser*

Her Garden

Under the tigers,
her Janie keeps whimpering,
my Lambie's there,
and no glossolalia of love
is going to put that child
back to sleep
with Lambie lying near
the lilies' orange tongues.
Three in the morning,
what an hour
to hunt for a toy.
She pulls on slippers,
robe, sees in the mirror
her face has been muddled
by bad dreams
and a startled waking.

The far corner of the tiny garden
looks like India in moonlight,
sweet pea a filigree
like the carved lintel
of a temple.

If only absolution
was like this, a land
the late-risen moon revealed
as an essential, yet gentle
gloss of the familiar,
a land whose intricacy assured
what's lost is here
whether or not
you find it.

Then she would be
what she is,
not the penitent

she's been turned into,
the one whose doctor
sacrificed her baby
to save her body's life,
but a woman in a night shift
who is blurred by sleep
sent almost at dawn
by her wakened daughter
into the dark garden
to find a lamb left out,
its heart-shaped head
and vulnerable haunch
lying in the dirt
she weeds and turns each day.

—J. C. Todd

Dresden China Boy

I take you down, dainty
globe-headed perfect you,
small monument of love

that I reach for,
you in the mirror,
dressed in your pout.

Oh, vacant baby in mid-gesture.
Oh, glass-eyed witness
in my dusty-rose room,

romantic roulette of my girlhood,
femme-eyed pretty boy,
my glazed baby-cake,

my Wolfgang,
my Friedrich.
Kiss me!

—Carine Topal

Madame Alexander's Amy

Two weeks after my mother's death, the doll was waiting under the tree, the blonde-haired Amy I'd dreamed over in the Sears Christmas catalogue, running my finger over the small photograph as if it would help me see her more clearly, reading her description over and over, the wish book consulted so often it fell open at the page where she sat with her sisters from *Little Women* as if the four of them were waiting for tea.

She was the artist I wanted to be. And so I put her name at the top of the list we mailed my mother at the hospital, never doubting her ability to grant wishes or make dreams real. It had to have been my father who went and bought her, but I couldn't figure out how my mother wrote the tag signed with her name, just that the doll was there that first Christmas morning without her, new doll smell clinging to my hand as I lifted Amy from her wrappings in wonder and fear, her hair pulled up with a black velvet ribbon, a white organdy pinafore spilled over her blue dress like clouds.

I wanted to love her, and in some way I did, though I was afraid of her too, unsure exactly where she had come from, so cold and hard and unalive in my arms, with sapphirine eyes that clicked open and shut, a doll that stared up at me from among blue paper printed with stars; a doll I couldn't ever really play with, worried I'd muss her with the grit of my life; a doll I once planned to bury in the backyard, and who watched while I was unable to do it; a doll who came like an emissary from the country of death to tell me that childhood was over, and she was the last plaything;

a doll I still have, sitting high on a shelf in the room where I write, her rosebud mouth clamped shut around the mystery of how my dead mother got her to me, her blond curls forever tight and unplayed with, one plastic foot bare, still missing a patent leather shoe.

—Alison Townsend

Playing with Dolls

Every weekend morning, I'd sneak downstairs to play
with my sisters' Barbie dolls. They had all
of them: Barbie, Ken, Allan, Midge, Skipper and
Skooter. They even had the little freckled boy,
Ricky ("Skipper's Friend"), and Francie, "Barbie's
'MOD'ern cousin." Quietly, I'd set the dolls

in front of their wardrobe cases, take the dolls'
clothes off miniature plastic hangers, and play
until my father woke up. There were several Barbies—
blonde ponytail, black bubble, brunette flip—all
with the same pointed tits, which (odd for a boy)
didn't interest me as much as the dresses and

accessories. I'd finger each glove and hat and
necklace and high heel, then put them on the dolls.
Then I'd invent elaborate stories. A "creative" boy,
I could entertain myself for hours. I liked to play
secretly like that, though I often got caught. All
my father's tirades ("Boys don't play with Barbies!

It isn't *normal!*") faded as I slipped Barbie's
perfect figure into her stunning ice blue and
sea green satin and tulle formal gown. All
her outfits had names like "Fab Fashion," "Doll's
Dream" and "Golden Evening"; Ken's were called "Play
Ball!," "Tennis Pro," "Campus Hero" and "Fountain Boy,"

which came with two tiny sodas and spoons. Model boy
that he was, Ken hunted, fished, hit home runs. Barbie's
world revolved around garden parties, dances, play
and movie dates. A girl with bracelets and scarves and
sunglasses and fur stoles—"Boys don't play with dolls!"
My parents were arguing in the living room. "All

boys do." As always, my mother defended me. "All
sissies!" snarled my father. "He's a creative boy,"
my mother responded. I stuffed all the dresses and dolls
and shoes back into the black cases that said "Barbie's
Wonderful World" in swirling pink letters and
clasped them shut. My sisters, awake now, wanted to play

with me. "I can't play," I said, "Dad's upset." All
day, he stayed upset. Finally, my mother came upstairs
    and said: "You're a boy,
David. Forget about Barbies. Stop playing with dolls."

                              —David Trinidad

To Be Blameless Is to Be Miniature

I'm making my imaginary dinner
        balanced on a drop of water.
    That button: it's a platter.

That raspberry-sized pillow on
        the playing-card bed.
    Of course no one eats.

No one sleeps.
        No one gets comfortable here.
    You cannot stand inside innocence.

But the mind moves from room to room,
        trains first on these dimensions:
    I slide furniture around.

I lift the shower stall,
        the book so small it can't be read,
    the wheelbarrow for an acorn,

all these little near nothings.
        No doors in this house, this open house,
    the only way in is pity.

—Lee Upton

Burning the Dolls

> *In 1851, in John Humphrey Noyes' free-love settlement in Oneida, New York, the communally-raised children, encouraged by the adults, voted to burn their dolls as representative of the traditional role of motherhood.*

That last night, unable to sleep,
   I prayed with my doll
     under the twisted-star
quilt, then held her close,

her flannel gown warming my cheek,
   her hair made of yarn
     brushing the tears away.
I sang her favorite lullaby,

then she sang it back to me.
   When the sky flared into dawn
     I carried her in my arm—
not crying now for anyone to see—

to my sisters barefoot on the lawn,
   circling the stacked wood, each
     bearing some small body
that stared into the remote sun.

And when the burning was done,
   when her white, Sunday dress
     was transformed to ash
and each perfect, grasping

finger melted upon the coals,
   when her varnished face burst
     in the furnace of my soul,
the waxy lips forever lost,

then I knew I'd no longer pray,
   even with fire haunting me,

    because I hadn't resembled
closely enough my mother,

hadn't withheld my burgeoning
   desire, so like a doll
     concealing what I'd learned
I burned and burned and burned.

                        —Michael Waters

A Shelter of Dolls

Perhaps it began with the ornaments—fabric scraps
turned into mushrooms and teddy bears, flowers, birds, felt
storybook characters accurate down to the last
extra half-hour. You never saw such a tree. Or generosity,
how they would go to relatives, friends, neighbors just
over for coffee. Casual. As though right then
nothing else mattered. As though
this one didn't take more than a day to make,
production line in her living room all year long.

Or earlier, purpose like security going
before four children were grown—or nearly, two
still at home when their step-father isn't
fighting with them (his own, she says, lie and steal), or they
aren't fighting their real father, thrown out of school—
their pictures in oils in the living room, forever small.

It's nobody's fault, she says, they're good kids,
they help with charities, Children's Services, church
bazaars she's always in charge of—all summer, rummage sale
items in her garage, collecting like Saturday re-runs,
some things don't change all at once.
The youngest has all the boys after her.

Myself, I remember an answer from church camp.
Thirteen, I asked why people grew up. To have
children, our group leader said, so they some day can have
their own children—all he left out
curing tomorrow like salt, the girl on the label
spilling it, each time smaller, her picture
within a picture within her own hands
smaller, smaller, smaller.

—Ingrid Wendt

Playing GI Joes

My GI Joe didn't care for camouflage,
that dreary mélange of green and khaki.
He preferred the minimal clothes that I created
with a pair of scissors and poor sewing skills:
hot little loincloths attached with a pin,
paisley ponchos that required only a hole,
a strip of red velvet for a headband or belt.

My GI Joe craved reconnaissance missions.
He would sneak about my sister's room,
raiding Barbie's boutique for fashion ideas,
trying on faux fur and elastic-banded skirts,
tube tops and a white-beaded bridal veil—
forays which seldom produced good fits
but occasionally spawned fantastic accessories.

My GI Joe was a gung-ho exhibitionist.
He'd rip off his Army fatigue jacket,
metal snaps rat-a-tatting like an M-1 rifle;
he'd strut that smooth plastic chest
as if his twelve-inch stature controlled the barracks;
then he'd drop his pants around the ankles,
displaying buttocks as solid as rocks—
an audacious tease for one without a penis.

My GI Joe learned to take a lot of pain.
He'd volunteer to cross into enemy terrain,
where he'd be captured without a struggle,
stripped like a go-go boy, and thrown into a cell.
Tied up, disciplined, tortured into a frenzy,
he was a master of man-to-man endurance,
revealing only name, rank, and serial number
as a sly grin edged toward the scar on his cheek,
a mark that covered so many of our secrets.

—Scott Wiggerman

The Stolen Girl

I overhear you educating dolls
arranged attentively in rows, soft voice
assuming every part and pitch to tell
the monkey's pranks, the ballerina's dreams.
We muddled through your stillborn sacrifice
for hospital insurance premiums:
Hearing compromised, brain's electrics prone
to short, balance skewed and speech expedient,
rough alphabet of grimaces and groans.
With you we learned how effortful life is
when human grants are lost, your sleeping rent
by dream or seizure extricating cries
as payment due from wayward revenants
like you, who'd trespassed in a blackened realm.
Some found in you confirming evidence
of prayer's power; others backed away,
indifferent listeners or overwhelmed
by death in life's array. Through therapy
each hard-won consonant and vowel built
a language from reluctant lips and tongue
until the fairy tale affliction—guilt
that silenced children for their parents' sins—
began to lift, like fog beneath new sun.
First signs, then words combined in sentences.
Now clocks align, the calendar unfurls
with names of friends, not specialists,
your book describes a recollected world
of wickedness and guile where witches rage,
the stolen girl they'd cursed to limbo kissed
awake, seeming unaware of damage.

—George Witte

Burning the Doll

I am the girl who burned her doll,
who gave her father the doll to burn—
the bride doll I had been given
at six, as a Christmas gift,
by the same great uncle who once introduced me
at my blind second cousin's wedding
to a man who winced, *a future Miss
America, I'm sure*—while I stood there, sweating
in a prickly flowered dress,
ugly, wanting to cry.

I loved the uncle but I wanted that doll to burn
because I loved my father best
and the doll was a lie.
I hated her white gown stitched with pearls,
her blinking, mocking blue glass eyes
that closed and opened, opened and closed
when I stood her up,
when I laid her down.
Her stiff, hinged body was not like mine,
which was wild and brown,
and there was no groom—

stupid doll,
who smiled and smiled,
even when I flung her to the ground,
even when I struck her, naked, against
the pink walls of my room.
I was not sorry, then,
I would never be sorry—

not even when I was a bride, myself,
and swung down the aisle on my father's arm
toward a marriage that wouldn't last
in a heavy dress that was cut to fit,
a satin dress I didn't want,

but that my mother insisted upon—
Who gives this woman?—wondering, Who takes
the witchy child?

And that day, my father was cleaning the basement;
he'd built a fire in the black can
in the back of our backyard,
and I was seven, I wanted to help,
so I offered him the doll.
I remember he looked at me, once, hard,
asked, *Are you sure?*
I nodded my head.

Father, this was our deepest confession of love.
I didn't watch the plastic body melt
to soft flesh in the flames—
I watched you move from the house to the fire.
I would have given you anything.

                    —*Cecilia Woloch*

The Doll Mother

When they have handed her from lap to lap
and pressed her for good-night;
have washed her pink and slid her in
like a silver spoon in flannel;
have shut her locket face
with a click of kiss; when she seems
to sleep tight, the way they want,
and dark swaddles the room
and the blanket droops under her thumb,

then the dolls break free:
clacking their porcelain eyelids,
creaking their rubber-banded joints,
pumping their cotton arms erect,
they swagger out of poses made for them
across the dusk; their wooden tongues
rattle Castilian, Lapp, Senegalese
in whispers like the chittering of swifts;
in wiggles like a hatch of spiderlings

they shiver, streaked in half-light,
rustle a soft-shoe she never invents,
only divines, dissolved in listening,
swimming away with them, squeezing her lids.
This, not imagination, is the gift
she practices, holding her breath
to let them breathe, the little ones
lined up, seeded with stories, deep
in the cabinet, as in the belly's dark.

—*Kristin Camitta Zimet*

Foresight

Kept from the sea, in a hotel with walls papered in clover,
you would insist you heard the water
as you stared from a sleeper sofa covered in sand, squeezing

the neck of your cane as I occupied the space your blind eyes
gazed into. Learning of your death was like
sitting on a ship without any windows. Last night, water flooded

the room by the Atlantic where its current used to murmur
under the voices on your audio books.
I want to know if the egrets still whisper in the trees, or if

the dolls with their porcelain hands and satin dresses still stand
in the room of your attic, smiling in that complete,
motionless way of theirs, hearing everything perfectly.

—Theodora Ziolkowski

Contributors

Dori Appel is the author of *Another Rude Awakening* (Cherry Grove, 2008). Her poems have appeared in such journals as *Prairie Schooner* and *Calyx*. She is a three-time winner of the Oregon Book Award in Drama.

Jeanne Marie Beaumont is author of four books, most recently *Letters from Limbo* (CavanKerry, 2016). Co-editor of *The Poets' Grimm: 20th Century Poems from Grimm Fairy Tales*, she teaches in the Stonecoast low-residency MFA program. She has a vast collection of dolls, four marionettes, and one dollhouse.

Chana Bloch is the author of *Swimming in the Rain: New & Selected Poems, 1980-2015*. The former Director of Creative Writing at Mills College, she co-translated the biblical Song of Songs and Israeli poets Yehuda Amichai and Dahlia Ravikovitch. Her poems have appeared in *The New Yorker, The Best American Poetry 2015,* and *The Pushcart Prize XL 2016*.

Meg Hurtado Bloom works as a copywriter. She has an MFA in Creative Writing from St. Mary's College of California. Her writing has appeared in *The Volta, Hidden City Quarterly, West Wind Review, Columbia Poetry Review,* and elsewhere.

Paula Bohince is the author of three poetry collections, most recently *Swallows and Waves* (Sarabande, 2016). She has been the Amy Lowell Poetry Traveling Scholar, the Dartmouth Poet-in-Residence at The Frost Place, a Fellow of the NEA, and a Hawthornden Fellow.

Karina Borowicz is the author of two poetry collections, *Proof* (Codhill, 2014) and *The Bees Are Waiting* (Marick, 2012), which won the Eric Hoffer Award for Poetry. Her poems have been featured on Garrison Keillor's *The Writer's Almanac* and Ted Kooser's *American Life in Poetry*.

Kim Bridgford is the author of nine books of poetry, most recently *Human Interest* (White Violet, 2016). She is the director of Poetry by the Sea: A Global Conference. As the editor of *Mezzo Cammin*, she founded The Mezzo Cammin Women Poets Timeline Project.

Jason Lee Brown is the author of a novel, *Prowler: The Mad Gasser of Mattoon,* and a poetry chapbook, *Blue Collar Fathers.* He is the Series Editor of *New Stories from the Midwest* and a contributing editor for *River Styx*. His writing has appeared in the *Kenyon Review, North American Review, Crab Orchard Review,* and elsewhere.

Leah Browning is the author of four chapbooks, most recently *Out of Body* (dancing girl, 2016). Her work has appeared in *Chagrin River Review, Fiction Southeast, Toad,* and *Mud Season Review,* as well as in several anthologies.

Lauren Camp is the author of three poetry books, most recently *One Hundred Hungers* (Tupelo, 2016), which won the Dorset Prize. She is the recipient of the National Federation of Press Women Poetry Book Prize, the Margaret Randall Poetry Prize, and an Anna Davidson Rosenberg Award.

Neil Carpathios is the author of three full-length poetry collections, most recently *Beyond the Bones* (FutureCycle, 2009). He won the 2015 Slipstream Press Chapbook Competition for *The Function of Sadness* and edited the anthology, *Every River on Earth: Writing from Appalachian Ohio* (Ohio UP, 2015).

Luanne Castle is the author of *Doll God* (Aldrich, 2015), which won the 2015 New Mexico-Arizona Book Award. Her poetry and prose have appeared in *Grist, California Journal of Poetics, Extract(s),* and elsewhere.

Kelly Cherry served as Poet Laureate of Virginia, 2010–2012. She is the author of twenty-four books, including *A Kelly Cherry Reader* and *Twelve Women in a Country Called America.* Her awards include the Bradley Major Achievement (Lifetime) Award and fellowships from the NEA and the Rockefeller Foundation.

Geraldine Connolly is the author of three poetry collections, most recently *Hand of the Wind* (Iris, 2009). Her work has appeared in *Poetry, Shenandoah, The Gettysburg Review,* and elsewhere. She has been awarded two NEA fellowships and a Maryland Arts Council Fellowship.

Nicole Cooley is the author of five books of poetry, most recently *Breach* (LSU) and *Milk Dress* (Alice James), both published in 2010. She is also the author of a non-fiction book, *My Dollhouse, Myself: Miniature Histories*. She is the director of the MFA Program in Creative Writing and Literary Translation at Queens College-City University of New York.

Gillian Cummings is the author of *My Dim Aviary*, winner of the 2015 Hudson Prize from Black Lawrence Press (2016). She has also written three chapbooks, most recently *Ophelia* (dancing girl, 2016).

Laura E. Davis is the author of a chapbook, *Braiding the Storm* (Finishing Line, 2012). Her poems have appeared in *Tinderbox, Pedestal, Luna Luna, Corium*, and elsewhere. She is a copywriter and teaches for California Poets in the Schools in San Francisco.

Susan de Sola is an American poet living in the Netherlands. She has published poetry in such journals as *The Hudson Review, The Hopkins Review*, and *River Styx*, and in such anthologies as *The Great Gatsby Anthology* and *Intimacy*.

Jessica de Koninck is the author of a chapbook, *Repairs* (Finishing Line, 2006). Her poems have appeared in *The Apple Valley Review, The Widows' Handbook*, and elsewhere. She holds an MFA from Stonecoast and is a former attorney.

Lori Desrosiers is the author of *Sometimes I Hear the Clock Speak* (Salmon, 2016) and *The Philosopher's Daughter* (Salmon, 2013). She edits *Naugatuck River Review* and teaches in the MFA program at Lesley University.

Caitlin Doyle's poetry has appeared in such journals and anthologies as *The Atlantic, The Southern Poetry Anthology*, and the *Best New Poets* series. Her awards include a Bread Loaf Writers' Conference scholarship, a MacDowell fellowship, and the Amy Award through Poets & Writers.

Denise Duhamel and **Maureen Seaton** have been collaborating since the early 1990s and have published four collaborative collections, most recently *Caprice: Collaborations Collected, Uncollected, and New* (Sibling Rivalry, 2015*)*.

Jane Ebihara is the author of a chapbook, *A Little Piece of Mourning* (Finishing Line, 2014). Her poems have appeared in several journals, including *U.S. 1 Worksheets, Adanna, Edison Literary Review*, and *The Stillwater Review*.

Susan Elbe is the author of two books, most recently *The Map of What Happened*, winner of the 2012 Backwaters Press Prize and the 2014 Julie Suk Award from Jacar Press. She is also the author of two chapbooks.

Roberta Feins is the author of a chapbook, *Something Like a River* (Moon Path, 2013). Her poems have been published in *Five AM, Antioch Review, The Cortland Review, The Gettysburg Review*, and elsewhere. She edits *Switched-On Gutenberg*.

Ann Fisher-Wirth's fourth book of poems, *Dream Cabinet*, appeared from Wings Press in 2012. She co-edited *The Ecopoetry Anthology* (Trinity UP, 2013). A Fellow of the Black Earth Institute, she teaches at the University of Mississippi.

Kelly Fordon is the author of three chapbooks and a collection of linked stories, *Garden for the Blind* (Wayne State UP, 2015). Her work has been published in *The Dialogist, Kenyon Review, Minerva Rising*, and elsewhere.

Kerri French is the author of *Instruments of Summer* (dancing girl, 2013). Her poetry has appeared in *Barrow Street, Mid-American Review, Waccamaw, Best New Poets, The Southern Poetry Anthology*, and elsewhere.

Alice Friman is the author of six books of poetry, most recently *The View from Saturn* (LSU, 2014). She is a recipient of a 2012 Pushcart Prize and is included in *Best American Poetry 2009*. She is Poet-in-Residence at Georgia College.

Richard Garcia is the author of three poetry books, most recently *Porridge* (Press 53, 2016). His poems have appeared in such journals as *The Georgia Review* and *Spillway*, and in such anthologies as *The Pushcart Prize* and *Best American Poetry*.

Christine Gelineau is the author of three books, most recently *Crave* (NYQ, 2016). Her work has appeared in *Prairie Schooner, New Letters, Green Mountains Review*, and elsewhere. A recipient of a Pushcart Prize, she teaches at Binghamton University.

Gail Fishman Gerwin is the author of three collections, most recently *Crowns* (Aldrich, 2016). *Sugar and Sand* was a Paterson Poetry Prize finalist and *Dear Kinfolk* earned a 2013 Paterson Award for Literary Excellence. She is associate poetry editor of *Tiferet*.

Meredith Davies Hadaway is the author of three collections of poetry, most recently *At the Narrows* (WordTech, 2015). Her poems have appeared in such journals as *Salamander, New Ohio Review,* and *Valparaiso Poetry Review.*

Marj Hahne is a freelance editor and writing teacher and the founder-director of The Avocado Sisterhood, an organization for women and girl writers. Her poems have appeared in literary journals, anthologies, art exhibits, and dance performances.

Jeffrey Harrison is the author of five full-length books of poetry, most recently *Into Daylight* (Tupelo, 2014), which won the Dorset Prize. He has received fellowships from the Guggenheim Foundation and the NEA.

Donna Hilbert is the author of six collections, including *The Congress of Luminous Bodies* (Aortic, 2013). Her poems have appeared in *A Year of Being Here, Zocalo Public Square,* and *Your Daily Poem.*

Akua Lezli Hope is the author of *Them Gone*, which won the 2015 Red Paint Hill Editor's Prize. She is a Cave Canem fellow and has won fellowships from the New York Foundation for the Arts, Ragdale, Hurston Wright writers, and the NEA.

Karla Huston is the author of *A Theory of Lipstick* (Main Street Rag, 2013) and seven chapbooks. Her poems, reviews, and interviews have been published in numerous journals, as well as in the *Pushcart Best of the Small Presses 2012.*

Julie Kane was the 2011-2013 Poet Laureate of Louisiana. Her poetry collections include *Paper Bullets* (White Violet, 2014) and *Jazz Funeral* (Story Line, 2009), winner of the Donald Justice Poetry Prize. Her poems have appeared in such journals as *The Antioch Review, Prairie Schooner,* and *The Southern Review.*

Susan Kelly-DeWitt is the author of *The Fortunate Islands* (Marick, 2008) and several chapbooks. A former Wallace Stegner Fellow, she has published work in journals and in national and regional anthologies.

Adele Kenny is the author of several collections, most recently *A Lightness, A Thirst, or Nothing At All* (Welcome Rain, 2015). She is the poetry editor of *Tiferet* and the recipient of poetry fellowships from the NJ State Council on the Arts and the Distinguished Alumni Award from Kean University.

Laurie Kolp is the author of *Upon the Blue Couch* (Winter Goose, 2014) and *Hello, It's Your Mother* (Finishing Line, 2015). Her poems have appeared in *Concho River Review, Iodine Poetry Journal,* and elsewhere.

Lori Lamothe is the author of two poetry collections, *Trace Elements* and *Happily* (Aldrich, 2015). Her work appears in *Canary, Painted Bride Quarterly, The Literary Review, Verse Daily*, and elsewhere.

Jessica Wiseman Lawrence studied creative writing at Longwood University. Her work has been published in such journals as *Acumen, Blue Collar Review*, and *Cease, Cows*.

Christina Lovin is the author of *Echo* (Bottom Dog, 2014) and *A Stirring in the Dark* (Old Seventy Creek, 2012). Her writing has been supported by the Elizabeth George Foundation, Kentucky Foundation for Women, and Kentucky Arts Council.

Denise Low served as the Poet Laureate of Kansas, 2007-2009. She is the author of twenty-five books, including *Jackalope* (Red Mountain, 2015). She is past board president of the Associated Writers and Writing Programs.

Mary Makofske's book, *Traction* (Ashland, 2011), won the Richard Snyder Prize. Her poems have appeared in *Poetry, Southern Poetry Review, Mississippi Review, Poetry Daily*, and elsewhere.

Charlotte Mandel is the author of nine books of poetry, most recently *Through a Garden Gate*, with color photographs by Vincent Covello, published by David Robert Books, 2015. Her awards include the 2012 New Jersey Poets Prize.

Jennifer Matteson has an MFA in Creative Writing from Fresno State. Her work has been published in *Tar River Poetry* and *Third Wednesday*. She teaches writing at Fresno City College.

Joan Mazza is the author of six self-help books, including *Dreaming Your Real Self* (Penguin/Putnam). Her poetry has appeared in *Rattle, The MacGuffin, Mezzo Cammin*, and *The Nation*.

Susan Laughter Meyers is the author of *My Dear, Dear Stagger Grass* (Cider Press Review Editors' Prize, 2013), and *Keep and Give Away* (South Carolina Poetry Book Prize, 2006). Her work has appeared in *The Southern Review, Prairie Schooner, Crazyhorse,* and elsewhere.

Kristine Ong Muslim is the author of three books, most recently *A Roomful of Machines* (ELJ, 2015). She lives in rural southern Philippines and serves as poetry editor of *Lontar: The Journal of Southeast Asian Speculative Fiction.*

Gail Newman is the author of *One World* (Moon Tide, 2011). Her poems have been published in *Ghosts of the Holocaust, California Women Poets, Calyx,* and *Yellow Silk.* She is a museum educator and a poet-teacher for California Poets in the Schools.

Sarah Rose Nordgren is the author of *Best Bones* (University of Pittsburgh, 2014), winner of the Agnes Lynch Starrett Prize. Her awards include two fellowships from the Fine Arts Work Center in Provincetown and an Ohio Arts Council grant. She is Associate Editor at *32 Poems.*

Jennifer Perrine is the author of *No Confession, No Mass*, winner of the 2014 Prairie Schooner Book Prize in Poetry; *In the Human Zoo*, recipient of the 2010 Agha Shahid Ali Poetry Prize; and *The Body Is No Machine*, winner of the 2008 Devil's Kitchen Reading Award in Poetry. She teaches at Drake University.

Jessica Piazza is the author of *Interrobang* (Red Hen, 2013) and a chapbook, *This is not a sky* (Black Lawrence, 2014). She curates the Poetry Has Value blog and teaches Writing & Rhetoric at the University of Southern California.

Andrea Potos is the author of six poetry collections, including *An Ink Like Early Twilight* and *We Lit the Lamps Ourselves*, both from Salmon Poetry. She has received two Outstanding Achievement Awards in Poetry from the Wisconsin Library Association.

Kyle Potvin's first poetry collection, *Sound Travels on Water* (Finishing Line), won the 2014 Jean Pedrick Chapbook Award. Her poetry has appeared in *The New York Times, Measure, The Huffington Post,* and elsewhere. She helps coordinate the Hyla Brook Reading Series in Derry, NH.

Jendi Reiter is the author of four poetry collections, most recently *Bullies in Love* (Little Red Tree, 2015). Her awards include a 2010 Massachusetts Cultural Council Artists' Grant for Poetry. She is the editor of WinningWriters.com.

Susan Rich is the author of four collections of poetry, most recently *Cloud Pharmacy* (White Pine, 2014). She co-edited *The Strangest of Theatres*, published by the Poetry Foundation. Her poems appear in the *Antioch Review, Harvard Review*, and *TriQuarterly*.

Susanna Rich is the author of *Surfing for Jesus* and two chapbooks. A Fulbright Fellow in creative writing, she tours her one-woman musical *Shakespeare's *itches: The Women Talk Back*. Her awards include the Presidential Excellence Award for Distinguished Teaching at Kean University.

Kim Roberts is the author of four books of poems, most recently *Fortune's Favor: Scott in the Antartic* (Poetry Mutual, 2015). She co-edits *Beltway Poetry Quarterly* and the *Delaware Poetry Review*. She is the recipient of a grant from the National Endowment for the Humanities.

Marybeth Rua-Larsen is the author of a chapbook, *Nothing In-Between* (Barefoot Muse, 2014). Her work has appeared in *The Raintown Review, Cleaver, Measure,* and elsewhere. She teaches at Bristol Community College.

Hayden Saunier is the author of two poetry collections, *Tips for Domestic Travel* and *Say Luck*, which won the 2013 Gell Poetry Prize. Her work was awarded the 2011 Pablo Neruda Prize and the 2011 Rattle Poetry Prize.

Enid Shomer is the author of four books of poetry and three of fiction. Her poems have appeared in *The Atlantic, Poetry, Boulevard,* and elsewhere. She has received two fellowships in poetry from the NEA. In 2013, she received the Lifetime Achievement Award in Literature from the Florida Humanities Council.

Lauren Goodwin Slaughter is the author of *a lesson in smallness* (National Poetry Review, 2015). Her work has appeared in such journals as *Crab Orchard Review, Kenyon Review Online,* and *Valparaiso Poetry Review*. She is fiction editor for *Diagram* and an assistant professor at The University of Alabama.

Emma Sovich is the author of a chapbook, *None of Us Know Any Stories* (dancing girl, 2014). She is a senior poetry reader for *Cherry Tree*. Her poems have appeared in *Fairy Tale Review, Caketrain, Salt Hill,* and elsewhere. She teaches creative writing at the University of Alabama.

Mary Ellen Talley's poems have been published in *Spillway, Poems on Buses, Kaleidoscope,* and *Quiddity*. She has worked with words and children as a speech-language pathologist and now works in the Seattle Public Schools.

Elaine Terranova is the author of six collections of poetry, most recently *Dollhouse*, winner of the Off the Grid Press 2013 Poetry Award. Her poems have appeared in *The New Yorker, Prairie Schooner, Ploughshares,* and elsewhere. She has received a Pushcart Prize, a Pew Fellowship in the Arts, and an NEA Fellowship.

Susan Terris is the author of six poetry books, most recently *Ghost of Yesterday: New & Selected Poems* (Marsh Hawk, 2013). Her journal publications include *The Southern Review, Denver Quarterly,* and *Ploughshares*. She is the editor of *Spillway Magazine*.

Maria Terrone is the author of three poetry collections, most recently *Eye to Eye* (Bordighera, 2014) and a chapbook, *American Gothic, Take 2*. Her work has appeared in such journals as *Poetry, Ploughshares,* and *Poetry International*.

Marjorie Tesser is the author of two chapbooks, most recently *The Magic Feather* (Finishing Line, 2011). She co-edited the anthologies *Bowery Women: Poems* and *Estamos Aquí: Poems by Migrant Farmworkers* (Bowery Books). She is the editor of the *Mom Egg Review*.

J. C. Todd is the author of *What Space This Body* (Wind, 2008). She is the recipient of a fellowship from the Pennsylvania Council on the Arts and is a 2014 Pew Fellow. She teaches in the Bryn Mawr College Creative Writing Program and the Rosemont MFA Program.

Carine Topal is the author of three poetry collections, most recently *In the Heaven of Never Before* (Moon Tide, 2008). Her work has appeared in *The Best of the Prose Poem, Greensboro Review, Spoon River Poetry Anthology,* and elsewhere. She is the recipient of the 2015 Briar Cliff Review Award for Poetry.

Alison Townsend is the author of two poetry books, *Persephone in America* and *The Blue Dress*. Her awards include a Pushcart Prize, Wisconsin Arts Board fellowship, and Crab Orchard Open Poetry Competition Prize. She is Professor Emerita of English at the University of Wisconsin.

David Trinidad's books include *Dear Prudence: New and Selected Poems* (2011) and *Peyton Place: A Haiku Soap Opera* (2013), both published by Turtle Point Press. The editor of *A Fast Life: The Collected Poems of Tim Dlugos* (Nightboat Books, 2011), he teaches Creative Writing/Poetry at Columbia College in Chicago.

Lee Upton's sixth collection of poetry, *Bottle the Bottles the Bottles the Bottles,* appeared in 2015 from the Cleveland State University Poetry Center. Her poetry has appeared in *The New Yorker, Atlantic Monthly, The New Republic, Poetry, Best American Poetry*, and elsewhere.

Michael Waters is the author of four books of poetry, most recently *Celestial Joyride* (BOA, 2016). He is the recipient of five Pushcart Prizes and fellowships from the NEA, Fulbright Foundation, and New Jersey State Council on the Arts. He teaches at Monmouth University and in the Drew University MFA Program.

Ingrid Wendt is the author of several books of poetry, most recently *Evensong* (Truman State, 2013). Her books have received the Oregon Book Award, the Yellowglen Award, and the Editions Prize. She is the co-editor of *In Her Own Image: Women Working in the Arts*.

Scott Wiggerman is the author of three books of poetry, most recently *Leaf and Beak: Sonnets* (Purple Flag, 2015). He is the co-editor of *Wingbeats: Exercises & Practice in Poetry* and *Wingbeats II*. His poems have appeared in such journals as *Decades Review, Red Earth Review, Pinyon Review,* and *Borderlands*.

George Witte is the author of three collections of poems, most recently *Does She Have a Name?* (NYQ Books, 2014). He received the Frederick Bock Prize from *Poetry* and a fellowship from the New Jersey State Council on the Arts. He is editor-in-chief at St. Martin's Press.

Cecilia Woloch is the author of six collections of poems, most recently *Carpathia* (BOA, 2009) and *Earth*, winner of the 2014 Two Sylvias Press prize for the chapbook. Her honors include the Indiana Review Prize for Poetry and a fellowship from the NEA. She teaches throughout the U.S. and around the world.

Kristin Camitta Zimet is the author of the poetry collection, *Take in My Arms the Dark*. Her poems have been published in numerous anthologies and journals, including *Poet Lore*, *Salt Hill*, and *Salamander*. She is the editor of *The Sow's Ear Poetry Review*

Theodora Ziolkowski is the author of a poetry chapbook, *A Place Made Red* (Finishing Line, 2015), and winner of The Cupboard's 2015 contest for her short story chapbook, *Mother Tongues*. Her poetry and prose have appeared in *Glimmer Train, Prairie Schooner, Short Fiction* (England), and elsewhere.

Credits

Dori Appel. "Losses." Copyright © 1985 by Dori Appel. First published in *The Poet's Job: To Go Too Far* (Sophia Books). Reprinted by permission of the author.

Jeanne Marie Beaumont. "Dream Doll in the Making." Copyright © 2013 by Jeanne Marie Beaumont. First published in *Court Green*. Reprinted by permission of the author.

Chana Bloch. "The Family" from *The Past Keeps Changing* (Sheep Meadow Press). Copyright © 1992 by Chana Bloch. Reprinted by permission of the author.

Paula Bohince. "Paper Dolls" from *The Children* (Sarabande). Copyright © 2012 by Paula Bohince. Reprinted by permission of the author.

Kim Bridgford. "Chewed-On Barbie" from *Doll* (Main Street Rag). Copyright © 2014 by Kim Bridgford. Reprinted by permission of the author.

Karina Borowicz. "Guardian" from *Proof* (Codhill). Copyright © 2014 by Karina Borowicz. Reprinted by permission of the author.

Leah Browning. "In the Chair Museum." Copyright © 2013 by Leah Browning. First published in *Eunoia Review*. Reprinted by permission of the author.

Lauren Camp. "The Model of Perfection" from *This Business of Wisdom* (West End Press). Copyright © 2010 by Lauren Camp. Reprinted by permission of the author.

Neil Carpathios. "The Afterlife" from *The Function of Sadness* (Slipstream Press). Copyright © 2015 by Neil Carpathios. Reprinted by permission of the author.

Luanne Castle. "Marriage Doll" from *Doll God* (Aldrich Press). Copyright © 2015 by Luanne Castle. Reprinted by permission of the author.

Kelly Cherry. "On the Work Ethic." Copyright © 2002 by Kelly Cherry. First published in *Poetry*. Reprinted by permission of the author.

Christopher Citro. "The Secret Lives of Little Girls." Copyright © 2014 by Christopher Citro. First published in *Subtropics*. Reprinted by permission of the author.

Geraldine Connolly. "Doll Suitcase" from *Province of Fire* (Iris Press). Copyright © 1998 by Geraldine Connolly. Reprinted by permission of the author.

Gillian Cummings. "Because a Matryoshka Doll Is a Nest Made of Eggs." Copyright © 2016 by Gillian Cummings. First published in *The Adroit Journal*. Reprinted by permission of the author.

Laura E. Davis. "The Doll Maker." Copyright © 2012 by Laura E. Davis. First published in *Mason's Road*. Reprinted by permission of the author.

Jessica de Koninck. "The Golem" from *Repairs* (Finishing Line Press). Copyright © 2006 by Jessica de Koninck. Reprinted by permission of the author.

Susan de Sola. "Frozen Charlotte." Copyright © 2013 by Susan de Sola. First published in *Measure*. Reprinted by permission of the author.

Lori Desrosiers. "The Room at the House in Croton" from *The Philosopher's Daughter* (Salmon). Copyright © 2013 by Lori Desrosiers. Reprinted by permission of the author.

Caitlin Doyle. "The Doll Museum." Copyright © 2009 by Caitlin Doyle. First published in *The Warwick Review*. Reprinted by permission of the author.

Denise Duhamel and Maureen Seaton. "Florida Doll Sonnet." Copyright © 2015 by Denise Duhamel and Maureen Seaton. First published in *Poem-A-Day/Academy of American Poets*. Reprinted by permission of the authors.

Susan Elbe. "Colleen Moore's Doll House" from *The Map of What Happened* (The Backwaters Press). Copyright © 2013 by Susan Elbe. Reprinted by permission of the author.

Patricia Fargnoli. "How to Hold on to the Magic of Fathers." Copyright © 1989 by Patricia Fargnoli. First published in *Zone 3*. Reprinted by permission of the author.

Richard Garcia. "Doll Heads" from *The Other Odyssey* (Dream Horse Press). Copyright © 2014 by Richard Garcia. Reprinted by permission of the author.

Christine Gelineau. "What the Children Know" from *Remorseless Loyalty* (Ashland Poetry Press). Copyright © 2006 by Christine Gelineau. Reprinted by permission of the author.

Jeffrey Harrison. "Operation Teddy Bear." Copyright © 2000 by Jeffrey Harrison. First published in *Poetry*. Reprinted by permission of the author.

Donna Hilbert. "Bad Times Barbie" from *Traveler in Paradise: New and Selected Poems* (Pearl Editions). Copyright © 2004 by Donna Hilbert. Reprinted by permission of the author.

Julie Kane. "Alan Doll Rap" from *Paper Bullets* (White Violet Press). Copyright © 2014 by Julie Kane. Reprinted by permission of the author.

Christina Lovin. "Paper Doll Ghazal" from *Echo: Poems* (Bottom Dog Press). Copyright © 2014 by Christina Lovin. Reprinted by permission of the author.

Denise Low. "Delaware Guardian Doll" from *Ghost Stories* (Woodley). Copyright © 2010 by Denise Low. Reprinted by permission of the author.

Charlotte Mandel. "After Torrential Rain" from *Doll* (Salt-Works Press). Copyright © 1986 by Charlotte Mandel. Reprinted by permission of the author.

Sarah Rose Nordgren. "The Only House in the Neighborhood" from *Best Bones* (University of Pittsburgh Press). Copyright © 2014 by Sarah Rose Nordgren. Reprinted by permission of the University of Pittsburgh Press.

Jennifer Perrine. "When You Ask Whether I Ever Played with Dolls" from *The Body Is No Machine* (New Issues). Copyright © 2007 by Jennifer Perrine. Reprinted by permission of the author.

Jessica Piazza. "Pediophilia" from *Interrobang* (Red Hen Press). Copyright © 2013 by Jessica Piazza. Reprinted by permission of the author.

Jendi Reiter. "The Fear of Puppets and the Fear of Beautiful Women" from *Swallow* (Amsterdam Press). Copyright © 2009 by Jendi Reiter. Reprinted by permission of the author.

Susanna Rich. "The Child Left." Copyright © 2008 by Susanna Rich. First published in *Eclipse*. Reprinted by permission of the author.

Hayden Saunier. "Flip Doll: Red Riding Hood" from *Tips for Domestic Travel* (Black Lawrence Press). Copyright © 2009 by Hayden Saunier. Reprinted by permission of the author.

Enid Shomer. "The Promise" from *Stalking the Florida Panther* (The Word Works). Copyright © 1988 by Enid Shomer. Reprinted by permission of the author.

Emma Sovich. "17th Century Ivory Anatomical Model." Copyright © 2011 by Emma Sovich. First published in *Pank*. Reprinted by permission of the author.

Mary Ellen Talley. "When Catholics Believed in Limbo." Copyright © 2008 by Mary Ellen Talley. First published in *Cascade* (Washington Poetry Association). Reprinted by permission of the author.

Elaine Terranova. "Secrets" from *Dollhouse* (Off the Grid Press). Copyright © 2013 by Elaine Terranova. Reprinted by permission of the author.

Susan Terris. "Broken Doll" from *Tale of the Doll & the Bootless Child* (Conflux Press). Copyright © 2011 by Susan Terris. Reprinted by permission of the author.

Maria Terrone. "How Dolls Are Made" from *A Secret Room in Fall* (Ashland Poetry Press). Copyright © 2006 by Maria Terrone. Reprinted by permission of the author.

J. C. Todd. "Her Garden." Copyright © 1992 by J. C. Todd. First published in *The Sow's Ear*. Reprinted by permission of the author.

Alison Townsend. "Madame Alexander's Amy" from *The Blue Dress: Poems and Prose Poems* (White Pine Press). Copyright © 2003 by Alison Townsend. Reprinted by permission of the author.

David Trinidad. "Playing with Dolls" from *Dear Prudence: New and Selected Poems* (Turtle Point Press). Copyright © 2011 by David Trinidad. Reprinted by permission of the author.

Lee Upton. "To Be Blameless Is to Be Miniature" from *Bottle the Bottles the Bottles the Bottles* (Cleveland State University). Copyright © 2015 by Lee Upton. Reprinted by permission of the author.

Michael Waters. "Burning the Dolls" from *Bountiful* (Carnegie Mellon University Press). Copyright © 1992 by Michael Waters. Reprinted with the permission of The Permissions Company, Inc. on behalf of Carnegie Mellon University Press.

Ingrid Wendt. "A Shelter of Dolls" from *Singing the Mozart Requiem* (Breitenbush Books). Copyright © 1987 by Ingrid Wendt. Reprinted by permission of the author.

Scott Wiggerman. "Playing GI Joes" from *Vegetables and Other Relationships* (Plain View Press). Copyright © 2000 by Scott Wiggerman. Reprinted by permission of the author.

George Witte. "The Stolen Girl" from *Does She Have a Name?* (NYQ Books). Copyright © 2014 by George Witte. Reprinted by permission of the author.

Cecilia Woloch. "Burning the Doll" from *Sacrifice* (Cahuenga Press). Copyright © 1997 by Cecilia Woloch. Reprinted by permission of the author.

Kristin Camitta Zimet. "The Doll Mother." Copyright © 2013 by Kristin Camitta Zimet. First published in *A Capella Zoo*. Reprinted by permission of the author.

Theodora Ziolkowski. "Foresight" from *A Place Made Red* (Finishing Line). Copyright © 2015 by Theodora Ziolkowski. Reprinted by permission of the author.

About the Editor

Diane Lockward is the author of *The Crafty Poet: A Portable Workshop* and four poetry books, most recently *The Uneaten Carrots of Atonement* (Wind Publications, 2016). She is the recipient of the Quentin R. Howard Poetry Prize, a poetry fellowship from the New Jersey State Council on the Arts, and a Woman of Achievement Award. Her poems have appeared in the *Harvard Review, Southern Poetry Review, Prairie Schooner,* and elsewhere. Her work has also been featured on *Poetry Daily, Verse Daily,* and *The Writer's Almanac.*

www.ingramcontent.com/pod-product-compliance
Lightning Source LLC
Chambersburg PA
CBHW020617300426
44113CB00007B/673